PLAY LIKE A GIRL

PLAY LIKE A GIRL

HOW A SOCCER SCHOOL
IN KENYA'S SLUMS STARTED
A REVOLUTION

BY ELLIE ROSCHER

VIVA
EDITIONS

Published in the United States by Cleis Press, an imprint of Start Midnight, LLC, 101 Hudson Street, Thirty-Seventh Floor, Suite 3705, Jersey City, NJ 07302.

Printed in the United States.
Cover design: Scott Idleman/Blink
Cover photograph: iStock
Text design: Frank Wiedemann
First Edition.
10 9 8 7 6 5 4 3 2 1

Trade paper ISBN: 978-1-63228-057-2
E-book ISBN: 978-1-63228-058-9

Library of Congress Cataloging-in-Publication Data is available on file.

For Asha
and all girls seeking liberation
through knowledge.

For Abdul
and all men who work for peace
through equity.

TABLE OF CONTENTS

AUTHOR'S NOTE

It bothers some foreign visitors that the people at Kibera Girls Soccer Academy (KGSA) refer to the high school students as "girls." Many teenagers in Western cultures are called young women or ladies, considering that seniors in high school have usually passed the age of girlhood.

But just ask the KGSA students what it means to be a girl and what it means to be a woman. Ask them which they feel like. Ask them when they think girls become women in their culture, in Kibera, in their tribes, in their religions, and in their own minds and bodies. The students want to be girls. Some of them were taught that they become women when they start menstruating, but they don't buy that. Some imagine they will become women when they become mothers, but they aren't ready to grow up just yet. The students want to be called girls because they are girls. They want four years at KGSA to learn, grow, play ball, and study.

These girls are mature for their age. Some are orphans who care for siblings. Others are pressured by parents to lift their entire families out of poverty. This heavy responsibility makes them grow up quickly. At too young of an age, they have to wise up to the ways of the world, the pressures of poverty, and boys. They will take the responsibility because they have to, but they know they are still girls. They are in no rush to become women. In a sense, these girls are fighting for their girlhood in a way that females in other cultures have been fighting to be taken seriously as women. Here, in this story, they are honored to be called girls. They are warriors, they are survivors, and they are girls. They want to safely act their age and claim their womanhood in their own time.

So girls it is.

INTRODUCTION

Our mission is to plant ourselves at the gates of hope ... the place of resistance and defiance, the piece of ground from which you see the world both as it is and as it could be, as it might be, as it will be; the place from which you glimpse not only struggle, but joy in the struggle—and we stand there, beckoning and calling, telling people what we are seeing, asking people what they see.

—VICTORIA SAFFORD

I first heard of KGSA in 2010. I was teaching theology and coaching afterschool softball and gymnastics at a high school in St. Paul, Minnesota. My co-teacher invited alumnus Ryan Sarafolean, the director of the KGSA Foundation, to speak to the class. The KGSA Foundation is a U.S.-based nonprofit that supports KGSA, a free girls' secondary school in the densely populated Nairobi slum of Kibera.

Wearing jeans, a dress shirt, and a corduroy sports coat, Ryan's brown hair was pulled back in a short ponytail exposing multiple small silver hoop earrings in his ear cartilage. He spoke loudly and emphasized points with large gestures, walking around the room and commanding the attention of the students.

Ryan projected a picture on the screen of a tall, broad man in a soccer jersey and jeans, with large hands folded and his body much too big for the student desk in which he was sitting. The picture captured the man in the middle of a gregarious laugh that showed bright white teeth and hid his eyes in a squint. This man, Abdul Kassim, opened KGSA for his girls' soccer team as an informal one-room school with volunteer teachers. In Kenya, soccer is still a man's sport, and more boys are educated than girls. Abdul was trying to change all that.

"The first time Abdul tried to close the school during holidays," Ryan told our class, "the students wouldn't let the teachers take a break. They didn't want a break. They wanted to learn."

He clicked to pictures of girls playing soccer and then girls huddled around a Bunsen burner. Enrollment grew from eleven students to one hundred thirty. The building kept expanding with the student body. The sports teams and clubs were growing. Grades were rising. Abdul is not a trained educator, just a man from Kibera who wanted his soccer players to stay in school. He lives next door to KGSA and has allowed the students to actively form the school. Ryan's KGSA Foundation financially supports the school, but Abdul calls the shots. It's working.

After the presentation in my classroom, I said, "Ryan, this is a great story. You have to keep telling it."

The student body I was currently working with was, in general, fairly white, affluent, and performing at a high level. Although the story of Abdul and KGSA seemed far away geographically, the girls there shared the drive to learn and grow that my students had. The KGSA story interested me as a woman, writer, teacher, and coach. It was also timely. The facts tell us that educating girls is both the right thing and the smart thing to do. Children are twice as likely to survive when their mothers are literate. A country's GDP rises as girls' attendance in school increases. People who work in international education and development have differing views on charter schools versus public versus private, coed versus single sex, boarding versus day schooling. There is not one answer to how the world's children should be educated, but listening to Ryan that day, I also knew with certainty that the KGSA story was part of the conversation.

About a year after we met, Ryan asked me, "Do you want to come see the school? Abdul would like to tell you his story."

I said, "Absolutely."

In the summer of 2012, I flew to Nairobi, Kenya. Day after day, I woke, sipped morning chai, and wound my way to and through Kibera toward KGSA.

Ngong Road, the main two-lane road leading out of downtown Nairobi, was perpetually congested. Conductors on *matatus*, privately owned minibuses, helped commuters onto their moving vans.

Teenagers walked against stalled traffic selling newspapers, candy, and lottery tickets through open car windows. I joined men in suits, children in plaid jumpers and oversized backpacks, and packs of sadly thin dogs walking through the exhaust on the thin, winding dirt path flanking the road. Small piles of trash burned behind the bus stops.

Prestige Plaza on Ngong Road was home to the outdoor coffee shop I used as an office because, more often than not, the electricity was on and the wireless Internet was working. Just south of the Plaza, a stretch of paved road led to the main entrance of the slum. Along the road's edges, women in brightly colored *kangas* sold plastic bowls, avocados, flip-flops, and charcoal. Soccer was played ceaselessly on a dirt-and-pebble field in the distance. The pavement ended at a municipal building where visitors paid to have an armed guard take them on a slum tour. Cars, mopeds, bicycles, kids rolling tires with sticks, and throngs of pedestrians jockeyed for space. I walked quickly and with purpose.

The ground was unsteady, littered with tire-treaded mud, sewage, and sharp rocks. Sounds of horns, reggae music, and laughter filled the narrow lane, made narrower still by rickety stands selling chips, electronics, and cell phone credits. A harsh stench seeped from a butcher shop where someone was burning hooves. Three neighboring salons plaited hair.

Past Kibera's first intersection, the market bustle thinned a bit; invitations or demands for me to buy various products were replaced by the attentions of curious children. Some of them pointed and shouted, following me for blocks and grabbing at my hands. "*Mzungu!*" they called to me: white person. There were hordes of children everywhere, with ashen knees and bright teeth. Moms tied napping babies to their backs, toddlers sat idle, kids with blank eyes sucked their thumbs, and little ones in school uniforms chased each other up and down the alleys.

At the top of the hill, the neighborhood of Makina began. Metal workers' torches sparked just outside of what would become my favorite restaurant. They sold *chapati*, unleavened flatbread, and beans for seventy shillings, less than one U.S. dollar. The boy who brought plates out from the kitchen had smooth skin and calm eyes. He was sixteen, a school dropout.

Makina is Muslim by religion and Nubian by tribe. The Makina mosque stands three stories tall, projecting the imam's calls for prayer. Mothers waited with jerry cans at the water tank across from the blue ablution block, where people who could afford it paid five shillings, the equivalent of six American cents, to use a toilet or shower. A few days a week, a team of men in sanitary face masks stood in the ditch before the mosque, shoveling out the garbage that had collected so sewage could flow freely downhill when it rains. The next day, without fail, the ditch was full of trash again, the smell of feces potent.

I turned off the main road and into a maze—winding rows of mud and stick shacks that inched toward intersections to create make-shift neighborhoods with narrowing walkways and sharpening turns. The noise level dropped, and the sounds and sights became more inti-mate, private, and domestic: women wringing out clothes, teenagers washing dishes, kids chasing dogs. I ducked under clothes dripping on a line, the smell of fresh detergent filling the air. Adhering to the Muslim value of cleanliness, the ground was swept to form a floor of clean, packed dirt.

Through a third gate and after seven turns, I saw girls in navy uniforms with plaid skirts taking a short break from class—buying oranges, using the bathroom, or just stretching their legs. They turned down a narrow passage with energy both focused and playful. The bright sunlight cast shadows on the expansive, brown dirt courtyard.

In this courtyard sits Kibera Girls Soccer Academy. Here, against the odds, 130 girls are fed, kept safe, and educated every day. Class was about to resume.

I met Abdul for the first time in the middle of KGSA's courtyard. He was even taller and broader than in his pictures. His hand seemed to consume mine during our introductory handshake.

Two weeks into my stay at KGSA, Abdul took me on a walk to see his childhood home not far from the school. On the way, he admitted that he had first thought I looked no more than eighteen years old.

"I thought you should be going to school here, not writing about us," he laughed. "But they are telling you their stories about being hungry, of walking through the forest to find water, of being beaten in primary school, of fathers who drink too much and mothers who die of malaria and AIDS and violence. They trust you. It's good."

In 2013, Abdul welcomed me back to KGSA and approached me as if I was a prodigal daughter returned, with a bear hug and boisterous laughter.

"You came back. Not many foreigners come back," he said.

I fell back into the work of interviewing, collecting oral histories, and observing. I was there to listen while Abdul was busy running the school. The faces that flashed across the classroom screen in Minnesota years before had become real people with real stories.

The KGSA school community believes it is okay to be from different tribes and religions. It's okay to dream of a life that doesn't include early marriage and motherhood. KGSA teachers will chase after a girl who gets pregnant and beg her to come back and finish high school after she has her baby. They will pool rent money for a girl who is orphaned so she will not have to move back upcountry. If a girl shows up with no pen, paper, or uniform, or if she is not capable of or interested in college, she will not be discarded. She will be taught. There is no waiting and no exceptions. The school felt like a haven, a team, a place to take a deep breath, a family.

"Then, slowly by slowly…," Abdul would repeat this like a refrain, in reference to the growth and change at KGSA. School buildings can be built quickly, but an effective education program for girls in extreme poverty takes time to build. KGSA, in its faithful patience, is transcending the definition of school.

This book is a compilation of stories from the family that makes up the school. They are not my stories, but they have become mine to share. I hope you will pass them along, as I have.

LIGHTING SLOWLY
PRE-2006

If I light up a piece of paper, it lights up so fast and then it's gone.
If I light up a charcoal, it takes a while to get warm.
It takes a long while to burn down.
Fast doesn't work in Kibera. To make change that is real,
we have to be at peace with moving slowly.

—ABDUL KASSIM

Dalifa woke early and was too excited to go back to sleep. She washed her face and put on her school uniform—a blue plaid skirt, white oxford button-up shirt, navy blue-and-white-striped tie, and navy blue sweater—before taking tea. Moving through her morning routine with quiet purpose, she pulled on white pants under her skirt and fastened a matching white headscarf just above her right ear, framing her round face. She flung her satchel diagonally over her shoulder to hang at her hip and grabbed lip balm, applying it generously as she ducked through the doorframe.

Math exam, physics lab, Swahili presentation, she ran through her day in her head as she walked. The streets were already bustling with people going to work, elders going to the mosque, and children going to school.

"Mbuyu!" she called to a man standing by the railroad tracks: Father.

He turned, saw her, and a warm smile spread across his face. After giving handshakes and pats on the back to the men he was laughing with, he joined Dalifa. They walked on together toward a narrow passageway.

"Dalifa, how are your studies?" he asked.

"Good, Mr. Abdul. Good."

"Keep working hard," he said.

The passageway led to the wide-open courtyard at KGSA. The school is a two-story, L-shaped building with a blue tin balcony and roof. In the courtyard, they parted ways; Dalifa climbed the stairs toward the library while Abdul turned toward the teacher's lounge. On the school's second-floor walkway, Principal Christine glided slowly from her office into the library in a long, flowing, bright yellow dress. Her dreadlocks wrapped high on her head in a black cloth, she carried herself with an erect posture, chin up and face calm. She entered the library with Dalifa and sat down next to Claris to look at the morning paper. Claris was grading math exams. Her eyes were fierce and her hair was tightly braided. She was intent on her grading. It was still an hour before classes started, but the library was full. Girls checked Facebook, played Scrabble, finished chemistry worksheets, and read.

Asha, the third woman sitting at the butcher-block table with Claris and Christine, documented a student's checked-out book in her ledger. A former-student-turned-library-intern, Asha wore a shiny black dress that accentuated her dark skin and tall, thin body. Instead of wrapping her hair, she had a dark plaid scarf dangling loosely from her hair down around her shoulders.

"Ashaaaaa," Dalifa said, smiling.

"Da-LEE-fa," Asha smiled back. "Are you ready for the meeting today?"

After classes Dalifa, Asha, Christine, Claris, and Abdul had a meeting with an architect who was helping the school design a dormitory. KGSA hoped to become a boarding school.

"Of course, Asha," she teased. "I was born ready."

Dalifa was born in Busia, a town by the Kenya-Uganda border on November 1, 1994, the fourth of five girls. She loved her father and followed him everywhere. He brought her to rural bars when she was little and gave her beer, telling her it was good for her if she had a tummy ache. She remembers it making her feel dizzy.

"The other men at the bar were nice to me; they gave me money for books. Sometimes when he was drunk, we would sleep out in the forest. The sound of the trees scared me. I couldn't sleep," she said.

"My mother told me, 'What you are doing with your father is wrong.' I felt in the middle because when I went with him, I took care of him. God sent me to walk with him. If he was stuck somewhere, I called my mother, and she would take us back home."

When Dalifa didn't go, he would stay away for days at a time. When his family started to worry, Dalifa pointed out all the places he went until they found him.

"I was like his guardian angel," Dalifa said.

"After a time they divorced, and the courts granted my mother the right to be with us. I missed him when they divorced, and I still miss him."

Dalifa went to a Christian school where she was made fun of for her Islamic head covering. On Fridays, they didn't let her go to the mosque. In 2008, she moved to Kibera to live with her aunt and go to school. At KGSA, where Muslims and Christians alike are supported, she feels comfortable, but she liked Busia better than Kibera. The houses are bigger in Busia, and the land is green.

"The housing facilities here are vulnerable, and it's dirty. We don't have water, lights come and go. The food is near the dirty places. We adapt, but it's not healthy. I miss my mother, my childhood friends, and the fresh air. There was plenty of fresh air in Busia."

It was no surprise that Dalifa's KGSA classmates chose her to represent them at the dormitory meeting. By 2012, as head girl, president of the Journalism Club, and the top student in her class, she was often the voice of the group. Although she would not personally benefit from the dorm, she was excited for her younger classmates. She knew that an extra free meal, dorm beds, and electricity would offer stability and help students perform better on their national exams. In Kenya, this month-long assessment determines if a student can go on to post-secondary school. Dalifa was proud that KGSA was on the brink of becoming the first free secondary boarding school for girls in Kibera. It was a dream that had been percolating for years.

Abdul Kassim, the man who opened KGSA in 2006, never imagined that KGSA would have a dormitory. In fact, he never thought he would work with girls. His original vision was to give the idle boys in the slum work to keep them busy and away from crime. Then, when he started working with female soccer players in 2002, he never thought he would open a school. The needs of the girls in Kibera have driven the dream and kept his vision alive. As their needs changed, so did his work.

Abdul Kassim is most happy when he is walking around the neighborhoods of Kibera. Usually, he can go only a few steps before someone calls to him. Sometimes, he yells an inside joke in Swahili and laughs as he continues on. Other times, he stops for a long time to talk. He will invite people to join him for his "walk and talks." Walking next to Abdul, I felt dwarfed by his stature and aware of walking with a great man. His hands, voice, smile, passion, and charisma all command attention. He walks silently for a long time until he is finished thinking and is ready to collaborate. Turning the girls' dream of the school into reality started with conversations in the streets of Kibera.

Abdul was born in Kibera in 1972 to a single mother named Rukiya. She was a tall woman with a huge smile and a laugh you could hear from a distance. She worked hard during the day, plaiting hair and making furniture covers from wool. In the evenings, Rukiya taught Abdul how to read and write. They cuddled in a shared bed every night when he was small.

In the 1970s, kids in Kibera had to prove they were ready to attend school by reaching their right arm over their heads to touch their left ear. Abdul was so excited to go to school, he practiced every night with his mother, reaching over his head with concentration and tenacity.

"Reach! Reach!" his mother encouraged.

Finally, in 1978, when his arms were long enough, Abdul started his education at Kibera Primary School. He loved school and prided himself on being the cleanest boy. Rukiya washed and ironed his uniform trousers and shirt. He always wore a nice tie. She worked hard to be able to buy him shoes that looked smart. Looking the part, he performed well.

After one year at Kibera Primary, Abdul and his second-grade classmates carried their desks across town to Olympic Primary. The school opened its doors to students in 1979 for the first time, absorbing children from smaller primary schools in the area. To get to school, he and his friends passed through a small river. Every time it rained, the water in the river rose, making it scary for the students to cross. Abdul's mother was always waiting for him at the riverbed after school. She flashed her huge smile at him as she climbed into the river. To Abdul, she looked like a giant carrying his friends one by one to the other side. Abdul waited to be last. He jumped on her back, and she carried him home to drink warm tea together.

When Abdul was in fourth grade, Rukiya went to Mombasa, a coastal city three hundred miles southeast of Nairobi, to get married. She left Abdul with relatives so he wouldn't miss school. On December 7, 1982—he remembers it was a Tuesday—an elder came into Abdul's class and asked his cousin, a classmate of his, to come into the hallway. His cousin returned to the room and sullenly approached him.

"Your mother got sick. She is dead."

Abdul was ten years old.

He went to live with his widowed grandmother Khadija, becoming the sixth and youngest child in her house. They all slept together in one of the home's two rooms.

Never learning how to tell time, Khadija organized her schedule around the birds. Every morning a group of white birds flew over the house and returned in the evening. When the birds left at 4:30, she woke and lit two open-fire cooking stoves called *jikos*, one for shower water and one for tea. She called from one room to the other for the oldest to rise. They woke, showered, took tea, and left for school in shifts. Abdul, the youngest, rose last and went off to school.

Abdul was no longer the cleanest boy in school with ironed clothes and smart shoes. Embarrassed and without the special attention he was used to, he became rebellious. But his rebellion didn't last long under his grandmother's watchful eye. Khadija had a temper and threw things when she got angry. When he snuck away from school, she found him and pulled him back to class by the ear. Khadija never attended school, but she knew it was the answer for her children and grandchildren. Abdul adjusted to avoid her wrath.

Khadija could still see the hurt in his eyes from his mother's death. She sold *mandazi* and made him believe that he was the magic ingredient. He got the first bite of dough in the mornings so that the batch would sell well at market. After school, he helped her make dough for the following day. She also sent him to a neighbor's farm in Machakos during holidays from school to rest and get fresh air.

"Keep healing," she encouraged him.

Khadija would not let him use the death of his mother as an excuse to throw his education away. By the time he took his primary school exams, he scored well enough to be accepted into a national high school.

Dagoretti High School was about twelve miles from his grandmother's home in Kibera, and he wanted to be a boarding student there. She didn't yet trust him and was worried that he would lose focus. Some of Abdul's classmates spent the tuition their parents gave them on other things and were forced to drop out. Khadija wouldn't let that happen. She made him commute, and she provided the daily bus fare. On days when tuition was due, instead of giving him the money, she rode the bus with him and paid the fees herself. Her strategic vigilance paid off. Abdul did well on his secondary exams and enrolled in the Central Training School, a Nairobi university specializing in engineering, communications, business, and information technology. He lived on campus without his grandmother's guidance. Physics there was so much harder than secondary school that he attended class daily and studied late into the night.

In 1991, Abdul earned a diploma in telecommunications and was hired at the Kenya Posts and Telecommunications Corporation, later called Telekom, repairing external telephone lines. The work was active, outdoors, and interesting; this proved to be a great fit for Abdul. He reported to the office each morning and spent the rest of the day in the field. The team was often overstaffed, and Abdul got sent back home to Kibera regularly. He was assigned to a nice estate where faults in the line were rarely reported, leaving him with a good deal of leisure time.

As more people moved into Kibera from rural areas to find work in Nairobi, the slum changed. Land that had grown food and trees was taken over by shacks. The Nairobi job market couldn't support the influx of people, and unemployment was high. The government did not adjust with proper infrastructure, so there was nowhere to use a bathroom or throw away trash. Boys who couldn't afford tuition congregated at the railway line in Kibera. Idle and bored, they got into trouble with drugs, alcohol, and crime. Abdul saw in these boys what could have become of him if it had not been for his mother and grandmother. He wanted to help them channel their strength toward something productive in hopes of making Kibera safer for everyone. He approached them and started forming relationships. He learned that they wanted work, and they didn't want to be bored. Abdul gave the group of youths the name Gange, which means "job" in Sheng, to give them a sense of belonging. Together, Gange decided to start a carwash for Nairobi commuters.

The carwash was up and running well within a few months. The boys were making money and feeling accomplished. Abdul wanted to teach the boys how to save money and grow the business. They weren't interested. They wanted to keep it simple—wash cars, make a little money, and spend it. Abdul was sympathetic. They had never made money before. Abdul supported the boys' decision to maintain the business without growing it. He told them that it was time for him to move on.

The carwash is still running after twenty years. The now-grown workers still call to him affectionately whenever he walks by.

In 2002, the same year his grandmother died, Abdul saw a beautiful woman in his neighborhood. A friend told him her name was Zakiya. He thought she was striking, with light skin, big seeking eyes, and an even bigger, warm smile. She had an easy laugh and spoke with a soft, soothing voice. She was a Nubian from Kibera who enjoyed a quiet and domestic life. They courted for a year and then married. Zakiya was supportive of Abdul's community organizing that took him away from home after work.

She told him, "I knew what was coming when I married you. I knew I couldn't have you all to myself."

With Zakiya's support, Abdul started looking for a new way to work with young people in the slum. He wanted to do his part to honor the mother who carried him through the river from school and the grandmother who traveled with him to pay tuition. He believed working with young people was the most effective way he could improve his community.

Kibera wasn't always so crowded and dirty; it hadn't always been so hard to find work and affordable food. Abdul and Zakiya's tribal ancestors, the Nubians, are from South Sudan. The British recruited the Nubians to fight in their wars. In turn, they were given British citizenship and stable jobs driving trains or working in the post office. The British settled the Nubians on the land that is modern-day Kibera in 1917. It acted like a military camp, a place for the families of active and former Nubian military. Every evening at six, a bell rang indicating that all non-Nubians needed to leave.

Abdul was born a decade after Kenya's independence in 1963, and his childhood home had a grassy yard with an avocado tree to climb. He went swimming and fishing in a lake that was full of boats. Sprawling farms received enough rain for two full planting seasons. During harvest, Nubians filled bins with surplus kale, potatoes, and maize. There was food for everyone.

By the 1990s, life in the rural areas had gotten tougher. The people upcountry saw the tall Nairobi buildings on TV and imagined good things happening there. Politicians called men to the cities to work, and the call was answered. Kibera was cheap, convenient, and within walking distance of the industrial area. Men moved into Kibera, built temporary homes on farmland, got low-paying jobs, and couldn't afford to move from Kibera into the Nairobi estates. Their relatives from upcountry also came, got low-paying jobs, and became stuck in Kibera. The cycle continued. Today there are sixteen villages in Kibera full of hardworking people who walk to nearby estates in upper-class neighborhoods, like Langa'ta, to work.

Nubians had been given their land in Kibera without documentation. In the 1980s, Kikuyu families who used to work for Nubian families started claiming land for themselves. When other tribes entered Kibera in droves during the rural-urban migration of that time, Nubians had no legal recourse to slow the overpopulation and deforestation. Big farms were broken up into smaller plots. At first, the Nubian elders were calm and generous—there was enough to share. "Okay, let it go," they said. "What we have belongs to God." Used to living together, Nubians started to congregate in the Kibera neighborhoods of Makina and Lindi.

The Nubians continued to receive rations of powdered milk and biscuits from the British well after the fighting stopped. They would save the tins from the rations and use them to replace their thatched roofs. Tin keeps out the rain better than brush, so the trend caught on. As more and more people moved into Kibera to attempt to make a life in Nairobi, the lush farming land, saturated with green trees, slowly was replaced by tin.

"We aren't lazy," Abdul argued, countering a Nairobi stereotype. "Kibera is abuzz at five in the morning, people running around trying to make a living for themselves. Kiberans make the economic system run in Kenya. We run the machines in the industrial area. We open gates, make flower gardens, cook, and take care of rich people's kids. The rich need this slum for their own survival. They get their maids, houseboys, and watchmen from Kibera. And then they underpay us, so we have to work long hours. There is no time to study. We know what we want, but we don't get the opportunity. My grandmother gave me a chance to study, so I wanted to do my part to break the cycle."

Although Kibera is no longer considered a Nubian territory, Nubians still feel a special claim to it. They have been there for generations. Abdul's relatives are buried in the cemetery in Kibera. He feels a special responsibility to make Kibera better.

During Abdul's transition from the carwash, another local leader told him, "There's a young *mzungu* I think you should meet."

Rye Barcott was a well-connected undergraduate student at the University of North Carolina at Chapel Hill. A tall man with dark hair, broad shoulders, a square jaw, deep-set eyes, and a kind smile, Rye first travelled to Kibera in 2000 to study ethnic violence before joining the U.S. Marines. In 2001, Rye cofounded Carolina for Kibera (CFK), which began with a soccer program, a slum cleanup initiative, and a medical clinic—all within Kibera—to break down tribal tensions and increase quality of life in the slum. With access to funding from big foundations and individuals in the United States, he grew a large network of financial support for CFK.

Rye and Abdul met and liked each other right away. Abdul was inspired by how much Rye was able to accomplish in Kibera as an American. He wanted to be a part of what Rye was doing with CFK. They were both energetic, optimistic visionaries. Abdul needed Rye's access to funding, and Rye needed Abdul's cultural competency and relationship-building acumen on the ground. When visiting, Rye would stay at Abdul's house, spending long hours talking about the potential in Kibera.

Rye hired Abdul as one of his girls' soccer coaches, along with Salim Yayha Sebit, another Kiberan. Robison Rider, an American, rounded out the team as a volunteer who came to help during the summers. Rye started CFK to address ethnic violence with sports, but Abdul thought soccer was also a perfect avenue to address gender inequalities in Kibera. At that particular time, it was starkly clear that women on the field were not treated equally.

Abdul, Salim, and Robison recruited young girls from around Kibera and started teaching them to play soccer as a team representing CFK. Early in 2002, when Abdul and Salim brought the CFK girls to the field to play, the boys snatched the soccer ball away.

They said, "The ball belongs to us. You girls can go home and wash dishes."

In Kenya, soccer has traditionally been a man's game. As a girls' coach, Abdul had a chance to show men and boys in the community and the girls themselves that girls can do what boys can. A girl can feel strong and in control of her own body on the soccer field. A victory for an athletic girl in the sporting arena can translate to strength on the street. Athletics becomes a staging for life itself; sports can bring about social change. Abdul was excited to use soccer as a vehicle for change in Kibera.

Abdul and Salim went around Kibera looking for girls who ran through the schoolyards with tenacity and confidence. One of the girls they found was Rose. She had a love of the game inside her, and she quickly emerged as one of the most talented girls on the CFK team.

Rose first saw women playing soccer on television in the World Cup. She thought, "I'm a woman. Can't I be like them? Can't I try?" Boys played soccer at her school, and she wanted to play too. She walked up to the boys one day at school and said, "Women are playing on television. We can do it."

They wouldn't let her play. So she took used paper and fashioned a ball and started playing alone. She stayed after school every day and played as long as she could. Eventually, the boys let her play, and they went to the schoolyard to play during holidays together. Each kid pitched in five shillings, six American cents, to buy a ball.

But when Rose came home from playing, her father beat her. He believed soccer was for boys and wanted Rose to focus on her schoolwork. He beat her daily, but she refused to stop playing.

"I asked God to give me strength because I knew soccer was my talent. I was not good in books, but I forced myself to go to school so I could learn how to write and read. I studied because I knew it was good, but I played soccer because I loved it."

Eventually Rose's father grew weary and stopped beating her. He never got to see her play. When she was twelve years old, he died.

Abdul found other girls like Rose in Kibera playing soccer barefoot with balls made from paper and string. He invited them to play for CFK, and their training began.

CFK was receiving large donations, so Abdul, Salim, and Robison dreamed big. The coaches requested money to take the girls to a private field to train, away from the boys' harassment. They requested funds for cleats and socks since many of the girls were playing in bare feet. The girls had never been outside of Kibera, so CFK requested funds to take them on educational tours. They wanted the girls to see life outside of Kibera and realize that staying in school was an option that could lift them out of poverty.

Rye denied their request. Undeterred, Robison donated his own personal money to the team. Abdul, Salim, and Robison rented a field for two weeks of intense private training. By the end of week two, the girls were ready to compete. Since they were the only girls playing soccer in Kibera at the time, they took on the boys.

At first, the boys beat the girls and beat them badly: 5-0, 4-0, 3-0. When the boys scored, they ran past Abdul and Salim with their shirts pulled over their heads, taunting them. The coaches kept their cool. They knew it was motivating the girls to work even harder.

Abdul told the girls, "Look, we are improving. We are losing by less. We will beat them someday."

He saw them work even harder at practice. You could see the determination in their eyes. They were starting to believe that they could do what the boys were doing, and do it even better.

Then the day came. The CFK girls were the only ones in a boys' tournament. The girls, ranging in age from twelve to fourteen, wore blue jerseys donated by a school in the United States. There was a lot of pressure on the field. A tiny tomboy nicknamed "Commando" answered a score from the boys in the first half with an impressively sharp line-drive goal. Well into the game, the boys got frustrated that it was still tied 1-1 and started playing more physically, with thrown elbows and slide tackles, and the verbal taunting increased. The girls played harder than usual, as if they could feel the win in their guts. With little time left in regulation, the boys had a penalty kick, but they missed wide. The game went into a shootout. The CFK girls knew they had a chance to win.

Every time the boys scored an overtime penalty kick, they taunted the girls. And the girls kept answering, back and forth. The boys scored; the girls answered with a score. Finally, one of the boys missed his shot wide. If the girls scored, they would win the game. Commando kicked the last ball, and it went in. The girls won, and the boys couldn't believe it. The boys sat on the ground crying. And the little boy spectators were rebuking them, "Why did you let the girls beat you?"

The girls looked at each other with huge smiles, a bit in disbelief, but they also stood tall, knowing that they belonged on the field. The little girl spectators cheered and cheered.

After that win, when boys saw the CFK girls going to a soccer match with their bags, they followed them to watch. Slowly, the girls were accepted and respected on the field. According to Abdul, being respected was the first win for the girls of Kibera.

While the girls kept improving at soccer, the coaches kept fighting with Rye about how CFK was handling money. From Abdul's perspective, CFK had a healthy stream of money coming in from generous individuals and organizations. Meanwhile, he was working with girls who worried about how to help their parents feed their siblings. He didn't think he should have to fight to get funding for things like food and shoes. Rye and Abdul fought bitterly over finances, and eventually Abdul, Robison, and Salim left the organization.

Abdul thought that was the end of his work with girls' soccer in Kibera. As when he left the carwash, he would have to find something new to put his efforts into. Abdul gathered his forty players, the oldest of whom was then fifteen, the group he had recruited and trained. He looked them in their eyes and told them he and Salim had to leave CFK.

"No!" they said. "You can't leave us! If you go, we'll come with you!"

The men talked about it. Together, Abdul, Robison, and Salim decided to form Girls Soccer in Kibera (GSK). All forty of the girls followed them there, bringing their blue jerseys with them. Salim stayed in a one-room home owned by his brother Duke. They used that house as their first office. Painted on the wall, to the right of an abstract figure of a girl kicking a soccer ball, it read: "Girls Soccer in Kibera: Gender Equality & Self-Awareness for a better future." It took CFK two years to rebuild their girls' soccer program. Once they did, a rivalry between the two club teams formed instantly.

For years, Claris has called Abdul *mbuyu*, Sheng for father. She needed a father figure, and he was it. Claris was short and strong and carried herself like an athlete. Her English was formal and crisp; she spoke with brevity and conviction. With the help of Abdul, she saw a path and stayed on it. Claris, along with Rose, followed Abdul from CFK to GSK.

Claris was born in Kibera, the sixth of fifteen children. Her father, a cobbler, alcoholic, and womanizer, got very sick with HIV/AIDS. The family transported him from Nairobi to his rural home where he died in 1991. As a young girl, Claris lived with a hatred and distrust of men because of her father. Her mother was left to care for fifteen children alone. She sold boiled maize by the railway line in Kibera.

When it didn't sell well, Claris and her siblings ate the leftovers for every meal.

As a girl, Claris played soccer all day long with a ball made of polythene and string. She lived on one meal a day—dinner after soccer. She trained with the boys and only realized she was different when she was not allowed to play with them in games and tournaments.

Claris went to the Kibera Community Self Help Program for primary school. She liked math class but didn't know she was supposed to study at home, because she had never seen anyone before her go to school. She went to school and soccer practice and then helped her mother sell maize. But even without doing homework, she managed to be one of the best and brightest in her class.

Abdul found her when she was in fourth grade and asked her to play for his soccer team. He paid her tuition when she was sent away for school. She was a goalie for GSK.

"I love being goalie because I'm in charge. The girls I'm playing with depend on me. During penalty kicks, I am the controller. It's on me to save the team."

Before GSK, Claris was shy. She watched girls in Kibera turn to prostitution and get pregnant at a young age. Not wanting to associate with them, she stuck close to her mother and had trouble making friends. She liked the girls she met through soccer because they seemed focused and driven. Abdul took them to tournaments outside of Kibera to play against the boys' teams. They started winning more often and gaining respect. When they had extra money, he fed the girls meals before and after games. They didn't, however, have enough money for more than one uniform each, and the jerseys didn't all match. Other teams made fun of them and called them "wash and wear" because they had to wash and dry their one jersey for every game. Robison Rider had some financial support in the United States, but most of GSK's money came from Abdul's salary from the phone company.

Claris smirked, "It was fine when they made fun of us because they also knew the mismatched team would defeat them. We were the champions in mismatched jerseys. One girl at a tournament called us street children, but in the next forty minutes, we won the match. We thought, 'The street children just beat you.'"

Abdul knew they needed more help if they wanted to grow GSK, and it came just in time. Salim and Abdul entered their primary-aged kids in a tournament with 150 girls from fourteen primary schools around Nairobi. Walking the little girls up to the field, Abdul passed a very old man.

He asked, "These girls are playing soccer?"

"Yes." Abdul said.

"I have a friend who has an organization called Sporting Chance. They work to help improve kids' lives through sports. Call him." And he handed Abdul a business card.

Abdul called Fred from Sporting Chance, and Fred asked, "Where are you from?"

"Kibera," Abdul said.

"And you have girls playing soccer?"

"Yes. We are Girls Soccer in Kibera."

Fred laughed and told Abdul that he had come to the right place. Sporting Chance had access to extra equipment. They donated eight sets of uniforms and eight balls and told him to give the items to eight teams. Abdul organized the eight teams and held the uniforms and the balls for them. Two sets went to the girls of GSK.

The uniforms were pivotal. GSK became a rejuvenated team, feeling as though they belonged. They felt special, confident, and strong. It was an affirmation of their abilities and a sign of having made it. Getting uniforms was a turning point for GSK. They kept entering tournaments and winning. Sporting Chance supports Abdul to this day. They are his longest-standing partner. It started with balls and uniforms and grew from there to include significant budgetary support.

Abdul's presence helped Claris realize that not all men are bad. He counseled and mentored the girls in more things than just soccer. Men in Kibera knew Claris didn't have enough money for food or new clothes. They knew she shared a small room with several of her siblings. She was highly vulnerable. When men tried to offer her a room or some money, she knew it could be a way of luring her into prostitution.

Abdul taught the girls to care not just about soccer but school too. Very few of the girls had parents, siblings, or friends who had gone beyond primary school. Claris didn't even know there was such a thing as secondary school. When she was in eighth grade, she asked Abdul about the girls by the railway line in matching skirts.

"They go to secondary school," he explained.

"Does it cost money?"

"Yes, there are fees."

"Then soccer will be my profession."

"Claris," Abdul pushed, "what if you break your leg tomorrow? You must keep studying. We will find a way."

Claris got 386 points on her Kenya Certificate of Primary Education (KCPE) exam. The national mandatory primary test takes four days to complete and is scored out of 500 points. Her score was high enough to get into a good secondary school. Abdul helped her find a sponsor willing to pay her tuition, but the sponsor wanted to send her to boarding school on the western side of Kenya. She was scared to leave home, preferring to stay with Abdul and her mother and focus on soccer. But GSK paid her travel fees and pushed her to study. The school was in a remote village by Kisumu, where she adjusted to the colder climate and boarding school life.

At first she was lonely. But she liked not having to walk a long distance to get to class. It gave her plenty of time to study. She also studied better, not having to share one room with all of her siblings. She joined the soccer and field hockey teams. When she missed her mother the most, her mother reminded her that graduating from secondary school would help her get a better job. With a higher salary, she could help ensure that her younger siblings had the tuition to go to school too. Claris's mother was thankful for GSK and Abdul for helping Claris find a different path, but not all parents had the same gratitude.

* * *

Faridah's mother didn't want her daughter interacting with boys on the soccer field or wearing shorts and removing her head wrap. Good Muslim girls didn't play soccer. However, once Faridah tried soccer, she refused to give it up. Abdul visited Faridah's mother, explaining that soccer had financial advantages. Some of the GSK girls played only for the free lunch after the games, until their teammates felt like sisters, and then they stayed to be around their newly found soccer family. Organizations hosting tournaments gave cash prizes and handed out free sanitary pads. Good players could earn scholarships for school.

When Faridah's mother couldn't make school tuition payments, Abdul helped. Eventually, Faridah became so good at soccer that Lang'ata High School paid her fees so she could play on their school soccer team.

"Because of soccer I got through high school. I was never sent home for school fees," she said proudly. "And I learned more about life from the team than I did back at home. Soccer helps you be mentally and physically fit. No one will abuse you, and you have another family," Faridah said.

Today as an adult, Faridah wears brightly colored dresses and head wraps with matching eye shadow. She applies shiny lipstick on her full lips, uses floral perfume, and has three small studs in her nose. It's hard to imagine her in soccer shorts and socks, sweating on the field, but she loves soccer enough to reconcile her religious beliefs with her passion for the game.

"I am religious. I pray and fast. Islam is against women showing their bodies. But I can't play soccer the way I am dressed. I'm not supposed to put on shorts and play in front of men, but this is life. Without soccer, I couldn't be the person I am today. I have to pray to God to forgive me, and God will understand. I'm not doing it to offend God. It is the right thing. I play the right way—not to attract boys, but for the love of the game. I can play soccer and represent myself decently. We leave it for God to judge," she said.

"In my tribe, the ladies are supposed to be housewives. But when I joined soccer, I knew that I could do what men do. I could go to school and get a job. Because we used to beat the boys, we changed a lot of minds. A woman can be president."

GSK started playing girl teams from Nairobi that had wonderful facilities and sent women on to play for the national team. As in 2002 with CFK, GSK lost badly at the beginning against teams from Nairobi. But they knew if they could beat the boys in Kibera, they could beat the girls in Nairobi too.

Eventually, in 2005, GSK won a big tournament. With each win, momentum mounted. In the final game, the girls were nervous and excited. They played with focused energy and cohesion. With time running out, the striker kicked a beautiful goal into the far right corner of the goal to win. Abdul, on the sidelines, rolled onto his back, covering his face and screaming, "What?!"

GSK was given money for the win. Abdul gave it to the girls and took them to the supermarket. None of them bought candy. They bought cooking fat and sugar to provide for their families, and Abdul thought, "Okay, that is some responsibility. When I give them the freedom, they make very interesting decisions."

Girls' soccer started getting more attention. Politicians and organizations sponsored tournaments with valuable prizes like uniforms and cleats. GSK won often enough to keep the team outfitted.

This same group of little girls who beat the boys, who followed Abdul from CFK to GSK, who started winning tournaments in Nairobi, came back year after year to play. As they got older, some of them started to disappear. Forty girls shrunk to thirty.

"Some got pregnant, some got married off, and a few went into prostitution," Abdul said.

The girls who continued playing were dealing with their changing bodies. They were under increasing pressure from elders and the boys in their families and community to get married and have kids, and they started carrying themselves differently under that pressure. Some made less eye contact and got quiet; others laughed less and didn't stand as straight. They had no money for food and could not afford tuition for high school.

One day, Commando came up to Abdul after practice, clearly uncomfortable. Finally she just blurted out, "Abdul, we need money for sanitary pads."

He gave her money right there on the spot, but thought, "What about the girls who are not coming to me? Who are they going to? Commando is daring, but what about the girls who are silent?"

FREE SCHOOL ISN'T FREE

2006

Giving birth [to children] is easy, the difficulty is feeding them.

—JANE AUMA, *SLUM SURVIVORS*

In 2005, GSK's three best strikers got pregnant. Some of the GSK girls were going to boys instead of Abdul for money to buy food and sanitary pads. In return, the boys wanted sex. Although this was consensual sex between minors, the boys often refused to wear condoms. Once stigmatized in the community as desperate, these girls also became vulnerable to sexual assault.

Abdul saw his players resigned to early pregnancy and marriage for financial survival. In order to retain them, he needed them to believe they had options, that there were other ways to get money for food and feminine hygiene products.

Organizations in Kibera attempted to address the sexual pressure young women were under, but Abdul wanted GSK to be more effective. One U.S. Agency for International Development (USAID) campaign, for example, came to Kibera painting *Sita Kimya* ("I will not keep quiet") on walls all over the slum. The program tried to inspire girls to speak up about rape, sex for money, and abuse. Their model involved gathering a crowd, telling a story, playing music, and giving out informational brochures and T-shirts, but they had no long-term commitment to the problem. No money went into education, counseling, or medical attention. There wasn't a *Sita Kimya* office in Kibera with lawyers trained to assist abused girls. There was no housing to protect girls who stepped forward. The money dried out, and the program was finished.

"The people who produced the paints and the T-shirts took all the money while the girls keep getting raped," Abdul said.

Sita Kimya remains graffitied on the walls.

Over the years with the GSK team, the idea of starting a school came up repeatedly. Abdul noticed that his players became more susceptible to early pregnancy and marriage as soon as they dropped out of school. School gave them hope for a different path, but few of them had families who could pay tuition for secondary school. When Rose's father died, for example, she didn't have money to keep going to school. GSK only won enough money at tournaments for a little bit of food. At age twelve, she and her teammates went out looking for work to support their families.

Abdul talked to the two GSK teams and asked them, "Okay, if we start a school, would you come?"

"Yeah, we will come!"

Salim wanted the school too. Salim lived at his brother Duke's house, which they used as the office of GSK. They decided Salim would live with Abdul for a while so the office could expand into a school.

In 2006, KGSA opened for thirteen students. It was one room separated into two spaces—an office and a classroom—on a busy Makina street right next door to a bar. Unlike most other Kenyan schools, they didn't have school uniforms or desks. They had two big butcher-block tables and chairs rented with Abdul's money. A friend of Abdul's bought one book for every subject. During breaks between classes, one girl would copy the book onto the board and the other girls would copy it from the board into their notebooks.

Abdul tried to run KGSA as a family where everybody depended on each other. The girls didn't leave school until well past dark. They knew they had a home away from home at this tiny informal school.

The next thing they needed was a teacher willing to work for free until Abdul found more funding. He needed to hire teachers who were either very rich and didn't depend on income or very poor and used to getting by on a low salary. The very rich in Nairobi rarely ventured into Kibera, so Abdul and Salim went out looking for teachers in Kibera. Salim found Joel, an unemployed primary school teacher. The second teacher, Teka, found them.

Before KGSA opened, two men working for Youth against Immorality approached Abdul on the soccer field. They explained that they helped form clubs within the schools, leading discussions around drug abuse, HIV/AIDS, and life skills. They wanted to expand their services beyond schools to the soccer teams too.

Abdul was impressed. "Yes, that's good stuff," he said, "but our problem is lack of education. My soccer players get pregnant and drop out. I'm thinking of starting a free school for them."

One of the men pointed at the other and said, "Teka is good at math and chemistry. He can teach."

Teka assured Abdul, "Yes, if you start this school, I'll come teach."

They exchanged information. A week later, Abdul called and said, "What happened? You were supposed to come."

"Has the school started?"

"Yes. I have one teacher and thirteen students."

The next day, Teka went to KGSA not quite knowing what to expect. The girls seemed old to be in the first year of secondary school. And, in fact, he learned they had studied at home for a few years without going to school after taking their KCPE exams. They simply couldn't pay for secondary school.

Abdul introduced Teka to Joel. The two-person staff was a little shaky—Joel was a primary school teacher and Teka wasn't a trained teacher at all. They decided (based on what subjects they had liked as students in school) that Joel would teach geography, business, and English, and Teka would take the rest: math, Swahili, biology, physics, chemistry, history, and religion.

If Teka thought the girls looked old, they thought he looked young. Teka was a slight man whose wardrobe ranged from argyle sweaters, grey dress slacks, and bright white shoes to red sneakers that matched his Liverpool jersey and scarf. He had shiny skin, wide nostrils, and a mischievous giggle. At first glance, the girls thought he was their age. It didn't take him long, though, to earn their respect.

Teka taught quickly, gave a good deal of homework, prohibited chatting in class, and sent them home if they arrived late or didn't come prepared. Within days, the girls were attentive in class and very serious. They could tell he was smart, but perhaps more important, he taught with high expectations and an energy and enthusiasm that showed the girls he cared. And he did. He was impressed by their commitment to learning. "So many girls in Kibera were raising children by age eighteen, but these girls came wanting to work on their studies," he said. Teka wanted not only to give them an education, but also to prepare them for the Kenya Certificate of Secondary Education (KCSE) exam, a national mandatory month-long exam used to place students in college.

Abdul passed by KGSA in the mornings on his way to Telkom. He would peek into the classroom and see Teka up front and the girls leaning forward taking notes.

"Everything okay?" Abdul would ask Teka.

"Yep," he would reply quickly before getting back to the lesson.

Over the years, most teachers Abdul hired left because they found jobs that paid more. Teka stayed. The connection he felt to the students transcended salary.

Richard Teka, who simply goes by Teka, was born in Nairobi in 1985. His father, Charles, met Teka's mother, Ephel, in the upcountry. They married, moved to Nairobi, and spent their early years living in Kibera with their eight children. When it was time for him to start primary school in 1991, Charles sent Teka and his mother back upcountry. They moved into a thatched house in the bush with one bedroom, a sitting room, and a kitchen. The roof leaked when it rained. Charles married his third wife in Nairobi and stayed there. Ephel relied on Charles to send money from Nairobi to support them, but the money didn't always come. Charles rarely visited. Teka slept on the floor, never having a bed. He sat outside his house, staring at the nearest railroad for hours, hoping his father would appear from Nairobi. He sang a song he made up about buying and eating meat while he waited. Meanwhile, his mother sold sugar and paraffin to survive, but she never found work that paid enough to support Teka and his seven siblings.

Hunger consumed Teka's childhood. He remembers tying a rope around his stomach in the morning before going to school because it helped with hunger pangs. Yet Ephel never let her children feel sorry for themselves. She had responsibilities in their church, one of which required her to distribute the offering money to the people in the congregation who had the most need. One day, Teka snuck into the containers for money to buy some *mandazi*. She caught him in the act and beat him with a cane from a tree. Afterward, she prayed to God for forgiveness on his behalf. "I had no problem with her beating me," Teka said. "It was my mistake. She was right; there were people in my church needier than me."

School was a refuge for Teka. The school was very far away, and when it rained, Teka stayed home from school because there were no bridges and the road would wash out. His mother lied to his teachers when tuition was due, promising to pay the next month, in hopes they would let him keep attending. One of his teachers, seeing his potential, gave him money now and then to buy food and kerosene for his lamp so he could read at home.

Many families were struggling to send their children to school around that time. Teka and his peers were in primary school during the period of the first Structural Adjustment Plan (SAP). The World Bank introduced SAPs as conditions that Kenya had to comply with in order to receive loans that were meant to move Kenya toward a free-market economy. Education and healthcare had been free in Kenya for decades. During the SAP period, cost-sharing was introduced and the currency was devalued. In some ways, these changes did help the Kenyan economy, but it also left families used to free education struggling to send their kids to school. Teka's classmates became known as a lost generation because so few could afford to go to school.

There were eleven boys in Teka's class at school, the perfect number for a soccer team. He much preferred books to soccer, but he couldn't let them play with just ten. Small because of childhood malnutrition, Teka was shy on the field. His classmates put him in the goal, and eventually he learned how to make good saves. But the classroom is where Teka excelled. Teka loved school and was a very good student, especially in math. His teachers asked him to do difficult problems at the board in front of the whole class, making him feel like a famous mathematician. He was the top student in his class from first to eighth grade. He stayed up after his siblings went to bed at ten so he could read in quiet. He put his legs in a basin of cold water to keep himself awake. When there was no kerosene, he held the book right up to his face to be able to see the words in the dark. Alone reading at night, Teka dreamed of attending the most prestigious, top-level boys' schools in Kenya. He wanted to be a political minister.

Teka did well on his KCPE and started boarding school upcountry. His mother gave him 200 shillings, $2.35 in American dollars, of spending money to last the year. He watched his friends, who got more generous allowances, with envy when they bought porridge, bread, and sugar to supplement the meal plan. At lunchtime, he raced to the cafeteria and went through the line before as many of his class-mates as possible. While the other 500 students went through the food line each noon, he ate, washed his plate, dried it, and snuck back into line so he could go through again.

His first year was hard. On visiting days, no one came to visit him. His sister back home was diagnosed with meningitis and soon died. Teka focused on his studies as comfort and was named academic chairman of his class. He loved school, but he missed home. When he finished his first year, it was decided that he would move to Kibera, live with his father, and go to the rest of secondary school there. Charles paid for Teka's last three years of schooling, even when he didn't have to. Again, Teka did well in the classroom. If you made top three in the class one semester, you didn't have to pay tuition the next. Teka was in the top three every semester, but he didn't tell his father about the fee reward. When his father gave him school fees, he spent the money on food.

Being good in school was financially advantageous, but not socially. Most boys goofed off in school and got bad grades. Teka, to save face, acted like the class clown during the day. He talked while the teacher taught and goaded his classmates. But then he went home and studied harder than everyone else. When it came time to take his KCSE, he did well, but not well enough. He needed sixty-six points on the exam for a government scholarship to college. He got sixty-four points. His father couldn't afford to send him to college, so he was finished. He refused to see it as heartbreaking.

"If I had gotten those two more points, I would have gone to college and gotten some boring office job. I got the job at KGSA because I was two points shy. I feel lucky because I love my job."

In Kibera, young women often stay in the home until they marry, a custom that contributes to families marrying girls off when they are very young. Young men tend to have a bit more time in their childhood home, especially if they are bringing in income. The day Teka graduated, however, his father asked him to leave the house. Suddenly homeless, with no source of income or food, Teka needed a plan.

Teka had a neighbor who ran a video cinema out of his home. He put a television at one end and benches lined up in the back. Teka took money from patrons and ran the videos. In return, his neighbor let him sleep on the benches after everyone left. For two years, he had tea for breakfast, skipped lunch, and hustled for shillings to buy dinner.

Teka became skilled enough at pool and cards to survive. Fifteen shillings, eighteen U.S. cents, could buy him some bread. Eventually, he started tutoring for 100 shillings a day, about one U.S. dollar. He did that until he found Youth against Immorality. He didn't get paid a formal salary there, but he did receive a bonus of about 5,000 shillings, or fifty-one U.S. dollars, once a year. That job led him to KGSA.

Teka and Joel were getting paid about 500 shillings, just under six U.S. dollars, in a good month. On several occasions, Abdul paid them what he could from his own Telkom paycheck because he felt badly that they were working for next to nothing. The budget for 2006 was $825: $200 from Robison Rider and $625 from Sporting Chance. Abdul knew he had to find more funding to retain his teachers. A few months after opening KGSA, he got an unexpected break.

Abdul went out one night to have a few beers and listen to some live Luo music at a bar in Kibera called The Big 5. He was talking to his friend and enjoying the music when a group of young white men walked in. They ordered beers and headed straight to the dance floor. The music was loud, the energy in the bar was high, and everyone seemed in good spirits.

After an hour or so, the tallest of the foreigners headed outside to smoke a cigarette. Curious about what these young men were doing at a bar in Kibera, Abdul followed him out to the patio.

He walked right up to him and said, "You're American."

"How can you tell?" the guy asked.

"I can just tell."

His name was Shaun Lamory, a junior at the University of Massachusetts at Amherst. He stood as tall as Abdul, but he was lanky, with pale skin and dark, intense eyes. He and his buddies were in Nairobi studying abroad.

Abdul and Shaun hit it off immediately and talked for the rest of the night. Shaun was the kind of big thinker who Abdul was always drawn to. Later, Shaun admitted that Abdul reminded him of his grandfather—wise, with a sharp moral code and warm goodness.

They talked about everything from the United States to development in Africa to the state of Israel. Amid the serious and stimulating discussion, they made each other laugh a lot too.

Abdul asked Shaun, "Why is it that when I meet Americans I always like them, but I don't like what your country does in the world?"

Late into the evening, Abdul decided to tell Shaun about KGSA. Shaun was immediately skeptical. He felt as though he'd been played and thought, "Oh, here we go. This is why the guy has been so nice to me. He thinks I have money."

But Abdul didn't ask for money. He was excited about what he had started, and that excitement was contagious. They exchanged numbers at the end of the night. Abdul wasn't expecting much; he was already used to people showing interest but not following through, especially foreigners.

He was surprised when Shaun called after a few days. Abdul met him at the entrance to Kibera and took him on a tour of the slum. They stopped on the railway that was constructed at the turn of the twentieth century by the British colonial government, stretching from Mombasa to Uganda. The tracks go straight through the slum. Small businesses line the tracks, and many residents commute via train to Nairobi's industrial area. There is one point on the railroad tracks where you can see the expanse of the slum—the densely packed corrugated tin roofs stretching off into the distance. On the other side of the track is a green golf course where politicians go to play.

Abdul pointed to the big wall blocking the golf course from the slum. Not too long ago, there hadn't been a wall. Then, during a water shortage, some people asked a golf course employee for water, and he gave it to them. He was fired, and the next day employees started digging a trench to build a wall. The wall still stands, so people can no longer ask golf course employees for water.

Shaun stood on the high tracks, staring at the slum on one side and the golf course on the other. He was silent, overwhelmed. His first words to Abdul, once they returned to the school, were words of anger and frustration.

"What can I do? What do you need?" he asked Abdul.

"We want to expand the school a bit. Put a bigger blackboard on the wall."

"Okay, I'm going to talk to my friends. We have some money. We can help."

"If you're going to use your pocket money, then you're going to be invested in the process too."

Shaun went to talk to his friends and brought Ryan Sarafolean, Ryan Burbach, and Brian Johnson with him to the school with a little bit of cash. Abdul took them around Kibera and introduced them to the people from whom they bought lumber and supplies. The four guys worked all day with Abdul, digging and building. By the end of the day, the classroom and blackboard had doubled in size. Their hands were covered with blisters, but they seemed energized.

Minnesota Studies in International Development (MSID), the program that brought Shaun to Kenya, combines six weeks of academia with a few months of on-the-ground learning through organizations. Shaun met Abdul and helped with the school while he was attending courses in Nairobi. Shortly after that day of building at KGSA, Shaun had to leave for his internship across the country in Meru.

MSID started in 1982 at the University of Minnesota. After an exchange at Kenyatta University, a professor named Michael Page brought students from Minnesota to Kenya and started MSID so students could study with Kenyan professors while living with families and working in justice organizations.

Dr. Mohamud Jama started working for MSID in the 1990s, lecturing to students about development. By 2000, he ran the program on the Kenyan side. Most MSID students do their internships in rural areas where there are many good, effective grassroots projects. Only the last ten years have seen a serious look at urban issues from a development perspective with the growing of slums.

Shaun had trouble with his internship in Meru. The nonprofit organization he was working for was not run very well. It didn't handle its money correctly. And when he saw children being beaten, he knew he had to get out. Without asking permission from the MSID program, Shaun told his house family he was leaving and called Abdul. "Abdul, I'm leaving my internship in Meru. Meru sucks. I'm coming back." And that's what he did. He left and came straight back to KGSA. Abdul and Teka invited him to teach the girls English. He taught the girls how to pronounce words and spell them properly. He introduced them to what an essay was. The girls called him Jesus because he looked like depictions of Jesus they had seen: tall and Caucasian with brown hair.

Dr. Jama was furious with Shaun for leaving his house family and job and acting rashly. However, he agreed to go to KGSA, and he was pleasantly surprised. He loved Abdul's vision and thought it was a great fit for MSID. He let Shaun stay. In hindsight, Shaun following his own code of ethics was the beginning of an important partnership between MSID and KGSA.

Dr. Jama is a light-skinned Kenyan Somali with a long face. He is simultaneously gregarious and proper, speaking with equal parts passion and intention. In 1980, he studied agricultural economics at the University of Washington. Currently the director of the Institute of Development Studies at the University of Nairobi, he is a Fulbright scholar, a Muslim, and a fierce advocate for women's rights in Kenya. He picks up his daughter and five sons from school every day so he can hear what they have been learning. He believes and invests in education for his children, the American study-abroad students, and the girls of KGSA.

After meeting Abdul and watching Shaun teach, Dr. Jama kept sending MSID students to KGSA to learn from Abdul. Abdul has appreciated the MSID interns. "Every time someone comes, they leave a piece of their heart at the school," he says.

Shaun joined Joel and Teka in the classroom, teaching English. During lunch break, he noticed that, instead of eating, the girls put their heads down and slept.

He asked, "Abdul, what's happening? The kids aren't eating."

"There's no money."

"Are you serious? They get here at seven in the morning and get out at six at night. There's no lunch?"

"Most of the girls don't have breakfast or lunch."

"Well, let's go get lunch."

Shaun took the girls around the corner to a restaurant in Makina called Fatima Juma. He bought *chapati* and beans for everyone. And that's how the feeding program at KGSA started. Shaun asked a couple of neighbor women to start cooking, gave them money to buy greens, beans, and *ugali*, and the women cooked it at a house around the corner. They all started eating lunch together. Initially it was fifty dollars a month for all the girls to eat lunch every day. He paid it. It was generous, but he just said, "You can't learn if you're starving."

You also can't teach if you're starving. Teka was unhealthily thin. Abdul remembers, "He looked like if he fell sick, he could die. I would tell him, 'Man, you need to eat.' He would be there from morning to evening. He had nowhere else to go. All along he never complained. He got his peace teaching the girls." Shaun bought Teka food too.

Abdul found out right away how expensive it is to run a school, even an informal one. Teachers' salaries and food expenses are continuous, and many donors are wary of a long-term financial commitment. Jerseys and soccer cleats are a one-time donation that can last for years, but KGSA needed food every day. Shaun's feeding program made a difference immediately. Abdul and Shaun both saw it.

Abdul and KGSA had also made a special impression on Shaun's MSID buddy Ryan. When their internships ended, Shaun went back to the University of Massachusetts at Amherst, and Ryan went back to the University of Wisconsin at Madison. Together, they raised funds to wire to Abdul so the feeding program could continue. Meanwhile, Abdul strengthened connections with Sporting Chance and the Rotary Club so that as more classes of girls started at KGSA, the food would continue to be free.

Before the feeding program at KGSA, some of the girls were having sex for food. In the poorer neighborhoods, girls hid behind booths where ladies sold chips in the dark of evening. Abdul heard the timid voices, coming from the dark corners, asking him to buy them food—chips, maybe a little fish, for fifty shillings, about sixty U.S. cents—in exchange for their bodies.

"These girls hiding by the food stands are so young. They're eighteen maybe, but they look forty. They get into drinking and drugs and have kids at an early age and don't eat enough and they look miserable. That's why the feeding program at the school needs to keep going. That one free meal gets them out of so much trouble," Abdul said, shaking his head and frowning, with heaviness in his voice. The faces of his most susceptible students are on his mind.

The lack of food had such a strong correlation to sex that Abdul started getting nervous about closing KGSA for the holidays. Kenya takes several breaks from school annually, and he worried that without the free lunch provided, some of his students would have no choice but to resort to prostitution. The girls who played on the soccer team in 2006 kept getting meals provided because the soccer schedule continued over school holidays, but about half of the growing student body at KGSA was not on the soccer team and was left to find food on their own when the school closed.

Linet was a beautiful young woman with serious eyes. She exuded inner strength and stillness, speaking slowly and quietly. In Kibera, there are different levels of vulnerability. Linet, despite her drive and intelligence, was one of the most vulnerable of them all.

Linet's mother Alice Nyanchama was the fourth born in her family. Her father couldn't afford to pay the tuition to send her to secondary school, and so she dropped out of school in the eighth grade. But she made a promise: "If I have a chance to educate my children, I will do so." Believing it was the only way to success, Alice told her children Josephat and Linet to take education seriously.

Linet was close to her father, a watchman, as she grew up. Some of her favorite memories of him involved days when he surprised her by bringing home new children's books. When she was eleven, though, he started to drink excessively and became violent.

"Let me handle this," her mother would say when he came home late. She sent Josephat and Linet to sleep at a neighbor's house while she fought with him until he grew tired and fell asleep. When this became a pattern, their neighbors didn't always let the kids in, and so they slept outside.

Linet was nine when her father got drunk and hanged himself.

"People accused my mother of pushing my father to drunkenness. They said it was her fault that he went crazy. We were left with nothing."

Remarried in 1996, Alice moved to Nairobi with her new husband, temporarily leaving Linet and Josephat upcountry with relatives who treated them poorly. To earn her keep, Linet woke up early to sell milk at the market. By the time she came home, there was no morning tea left. She often went without lunch. Her grandmother had a temper and often hit Linet as punishment for the smallest of offenses.

"School helped me forget home for a few hours," she said.

Linet and Josephat were inseparable, walking to and from school together. At night, he helped her with her homework, and they both did well in class.

Their mother moved them to Nairobi in 1997, where their struggles continued. Her stepfather had another family to provide for, and he cared for them first. Alice found scholarships to pay for primary school tuition, but she struggled to pay rent and buy food.

The neighborhood gossip came to a consensus: "She will not make it. Those children are going to end up in the streets."

The primary school Linet attended was overcrowded with students. Linet had a teacher who was especially harsh. "If I got seventy-eight and the next time seventy-four [on a test], I got caned. She hit the back of my legs with plastic handles." They had brown uniforms to match the dust that got stuck in their clothes and eyelashes on the walk home. She felt like dirt and was called dirty, but she had no choice of where she went to school. Primary education was not yet free in Kenya.

Complaining to her mother did no good. "I thought you wanted knowledge. We don't know what tomorrow will bring. Go get knowledge," Alice harped.

Josephat graduated primary school at the top his class with a high exam score of 362. Seeing his potential, a neighbor offered to pay his tuition for secondary school. When Linet graduated, there were no offers from benefactors, and there was no money for tuition. She stayed home.

Then, one day in 2006, Linet's mother came home from her vegetable stand with good news. Alice had been selling vegetables to Abdul for years. Abdul told Alice about the school he had started for his soccer team, and he invited Linet to join.

The very next day, Linet smiled at her mother and said, "I'm going to school."

She walked down the main road. On the hill, past the metal workers, next to a bar, there was a blue painting on the wall of a girl sitting at a desk. She entered KGSA with no books, pens, or uniform. She paused in the doorway, disappointed. She imagined a big school with beautiful desks, but this was a small room with a table and a few chairs. She took a deep breath and walked in, deciding to stay.

She was surprised when Teka walked in. He was slight, but tough. "I cooperated with him because I didn't want to get sent home. I wanted to study. He was a good teacher, especially in chemistry."

Commando was Linet's neighbor in Kibera. When they were small, she had taught Linet how to play soccer and juggle. The soccer girls like Rose and Commando got close with the girls who filtered in from the neighborhood like Linet. The pressure to drop out, get married, and have children was constant, and they supported each other through it. In Kibera, girls who couldn't pay tuition started working or got married so they would not be a continued financial burden on their families. What KGSA was trying to do was new, and the girls felt it. They were made fun of for going to a "mud school."

Because the students were all girls and the teachers were men, they also were accused of sexual impropriety. At the worst, the girls had stones thrown at them. They fought back by showing up to KGSA every day to study. They reminded each other that KGSA would help them be successful and build a good life, even on days when they didn't quite believe it.

Even with these daily reminders, some of the girls dropped out. Some got pregnant—by their boyfriends, by neighbors who gave them money to buy menstrual pads, some from being raped. When her friends got pregnant and dropped out, people looked at Linet and said, "She's next." The school was doing its best to present a new option, but life was tough. When men offered Linet money for sex, she'd lie and tell them she had enough money. She kept saying no, never got a boyfriend, and put her hope in the school.

By the end of 2006, KGSA had grown to twenty-six students. Teka and Joel were joined on the staff by Salim, the soccer coach who had defected from CFK with Abdul, and Salim's nephew Luqman. The school's reputation was spreading, so Abdul anticipated the student body doubling with a new incoming class. The school's budget had to double too.

Salim and Abdul started having money problems. Robison, the American who helped them leave CFK, was still a major source of money for KGSA, bringing computers and cameras to the school. Abdul and Salim each got a laptop from Robison, and Abdul expected the rest of the equipment to go to KGSA. With the exception of one laptop and one camera, Salim sold the equipment and kept the money for himself. The three men set up a bank account, but Robison didn't use it. He sent money through Western Union straight to Salim. Abdul was kept out of the loop.

"My idea had always been to start a family. But Salim was being greedy. He started bossing people around like it was his school."

Abdul proposed to Salim that KGSA split up into two distinct departments. Robison and Salim could run the soccer program and

Abdul and Teka could run the school. Salim agreed. Abdul told the teachers, "Salim isn't your boss. Teka's your boss. Teka and I are running the school." Abdul was still working at Telkom fulltime, so Teka became the principal at age twenty-two.

Dr. Jama sent a young woman named Jamie Clearfield to KGSA for her MSID internship because of her interest in international education. Jamie signed on for a full academic year in Kenya. The granddaughter of an Auschwitz survivor, she was a slender, pale woman with thick, dark hair. She spoke quietly and carefully, with surprising wisdom and compelling calm.

Like Linet, Jamie had pictured a large school building made of brick. When she saw KGSA for the first time, she was surprised that it was neither. In fact, it wasn't unique in any particular way. The classroom was hot, unless it was raining, in which case it was freezing. The school was right beside a drainage ditch, so the stench was distracting, as were the incessant sounds of Reggae bass, sparking metal, and bartering at the neighboring market.

Teka asked Jamie to teach Kenyan history and government, topics about which she knew very little. She wasn't used to teaching the way the girls were used to learning. Teachers spent breaks copying the textbook onto the board so the girls could then copy it into their notebooks. They expected lectures that required memorization, but no discussion or critical thinking. When Jamie asked the girls questions, she got blank stares in response.

But the girls loved Jamie. They thought she was beautiful and enjoyed playing with her soft hair. They got in the habit of absent-mindedly stroking her forearm. She went with them to their homes to see where they lived and to meet their families. Elizabeth, nicknamed Queen by Shaun because of her regal attitude, lived with relatives and was not treated well. Priscah, on the other hand, had a very supportive family; they just couldn't pay for another school. KGSA was a safe haven for them both for different reasons.

Part of Jamie's MSID experience was researching perceptions of urban poverty in different sections of Nairobi. While she walked around Kibera asking people to take her survey, she met a woman named Agnes selling vegetables.

"You are so small. Of course I will take your survey."

In the United States, it's common to leave home when you're eighteen. In Kenya, you may go away to boarding school, but for cultural and practical reasons, you don't often live independently until you get married. Agnes, surprised at how young Jamie was as an independent woman, said, "You are so far away from home! I'm now your Kibera momma. What else are you doing here?"

"I'm working for a girls' school in Kibera."

"A girls' school? I'm caring for Christine, my niece, who is an orphan. She just finished primary."

"Come to the school tomorrow and we'll talk."

Christine enrolled at KGSA, and Agnes started cooking for the school. More girls like Christine meant a need for more teachers and food, which meant KGSA needed more money. Salim's brother Duke, who owned the KGSA school building, had connections. He wrote a proposal to the Dutch Embassy for one million shillings, about $12,000 U.S dollars, asking for food, clothing, books, computers, lab chemicals, and teachers' allowances. The money came and went straight into Duke's account. He bought a few chemicals and some equipment. He gave the six teachers 10,000 shillings a month—$117 U.S. dollars—to split. And that was it.

A month later, Duke called a meeting. He told Abdul, "These kids must pay tuition. There is nothing in this world for free."

He wanted to charge students 1,000 shillings—about twelve U.S. dollars—to pay the teachers. Initially, the teachers liked the idea, hoping it would make for a steadier paycheck. Teka said no. Abdul said no. They knew the girls couldn't pay.

Abdul and Jamie took several long, tense walks around Kibera together. He wasn't sure what to do. He understood the logic behind charging tuition to pay teacher's salaries. He didn't know where they would move if he left Duke's place. It was a breaking point for the school. He didn't know where the money would come from, but charging tuition would change the mission and soul of the school. It was always supposed to be a free secondary school for girls.

Jamie told Shaun, who told Ryan the news, and they were both shocked. They said, "We'll find a way to support you; just make this thing right."

Abdul decided in the end to bring it to the girls. The school was their idea; they would understand the reality of the situation. He called a meeting on a Saturday morning, made sure there were no teachers in the room, and laid it all out. "Duke wants to start charging tuition. He owns the building. If I disagree, we're going to have to move the school," Abdul said.

Queen spoke up. "If you charge tuition, you're basically killing us. If we don't have education, we're dead. We don't have money for tuition." Unlike many of the girls who carried timidity and sadness, Queen had fire and wit inside her. Short and stocky with Kikuyu features, she wore her hair short, had small stud earrings, and a black hoodie with "Linkin Park" in white block letters across the chest. Her coy smile brought her classmates and teachers to laughter easily. She struggled academically at KGSA but wanted to continue.

Abdul decided, "Okay, we're going to stick to what we started with. We are a free school for girls. We will find a space. You can stay here with Duke, or you can come with me."

After the meeting, Abdul and Jamie went on a walk to talk about their options. Abdul decided to go to his family first to ask for help. They went to see Konga, the sister of Abdul's grandmother.

"My school has been taken away from me," Abdul told her.

She said, "Abdul, you have a home here. The field is for you. You have your place. Build here. Before she died, Khadija told me to hold onto the land until you were mature."

Abdul told Duke he could charge fees at his school, but he was leaving with Jamie and Teka to build a new school on Konga's land that would offer education for free.

They had the land, but they still needed money to construct the building. It was almost Christmas, so they put the girls' tie-dying skills to the test. The girls had learned how to tie-dye at an HIV-prevention program the soccer team had attended. The ones who knew how taught the girls who did not, and then they went to work making huge, colorful tie-dyed pieces of fabric for tablecloths and runners. Jamie and her MSID friends sold them to family and friends for Christmas and Hanukkah gifts. Shaun and Ryan did the same. In the month of December, they raised the $1,000 necessary to construct two basic mud-and-stick classrooms for the January 2007 school term.

At the ribbon-cutting ceremony on December 13th, 2006, the girls dug the first hole. In the ceremonial groundbreaking, they accidentally hit a water pipe and got a head start on making mud. The ceremony was followed by a soccer game. Abdul hired local kids and construction workers to build until the funds ran out. They started with compacted mud. As more money came in from the United States, two of the four mud walls were encased in cement for stability.

Abdul's relatives stood by, eyeing the new project on land that could have been theirs. Konga stood guard as well, watching the school-building project day in and day out. She said to the skeptical relatives, "I'm the last one remaining. The last one of the owners of this plot, and I have decided this is going to be a school. Does anyone have a problem with that?" She continued in Nubian while Abdul translated, "We all need to learn. You need to learn. I need to learn. These girls need to learn, so we build a school."

School was supposed to start on January 5th, but construction was slow.

"Maybe we should postpone opening school for a week," Abdul said.

Jamie said, "No. We're opening the school on the 5th. We'll build until we can't. We'll learn under a tree if we have to, but let's open with the rest of the schools on time."

Abdul agreed that starting on time would help make the girls feel like their school was more legitimate. He went back to the girls and announced, "We're moving. Who wants to move with us?"

All but one of the girls followed Abdul to the free school in the new location. Teka, Salim, and Luqman came too. Joel stayed with Duke, and within two weeks, the school at Duke's house closed for good.

On the 5th of January, 2007, the new and improved KGSA opened. The returning students entered their second year and new secondary students started their first year. The school would be in a constant state of growth from that day forward. The cement was not completely poured. Abdul used his Telkom salary to buy butcher-block tables and rent chairs. The floor was loose rock. There weren't enough desks for the incoming students. The girls said they would sit on the floor. They just wanted to learn.

Konga taught when they were short of teachers. During break time, the girls went to her room to visit her. She was happy being near the kids, and she oversaw the comings and goings of the school until her death in September of 2007.

"You did this," Abdul reminded the second-year students, brimming with excitement on the first day of school. "Your crafts brought in the money. You built the school. We are doing this together. We took a stance. Nothing is going to stop us now."

EDUCATING THE GIRL CHILD
2007

Educating a woman is educating a family, a community, and the nation.
—AFRICAN PROVERB

The incoming class in 2007 was academically competitive with each other. Abdul and Teka saw this as an advantage and played up the competition. At the end of the term, they had a ceremony naming the top scorers in each discipline and the three students with the top composite grades. Violet was named second in the class. Mercyline was number one. The teachers pushed Violet. "You have to work very hard," Teka told her. "We want to see you defeat this girl. Don't let her relax in that position. You have to push her so she will work harder and you will work harder." Violet studied late into the evenings. And at the end of the next term, she was at the top of the class and Mercyline was number two.

Violet walked up to the crying Mercyline and said, "Don't cry. I must defeat you. Next time, you defeat me. We will work hard together."

Violet had a round face and big, searching eyes. A great storyteller, her laugh was infectious and boisterous. She seemed to understand that hope cannot be passive, that only the hardest workers can have the audacity to hope. The road to graduation was long, but she saw it and knew she was on it. Abdul worked to keep the school open, without tuition and with free lunch, knowing what can happen when a hardworking girl like Violet is given access and opportunity.

Violet grew up in rural Kenya. Her father passed away when she was in the sixth grade. Her mother sent her to live with her aunt in Kibera to finish primary school. She contracted malaria in Kibera and was sick for weeks. She recovered and finished grade school, but when it came to secondary school, there was not enough money.

"In rural Kenya, we went to school in bare feet. In Kibera, we needed shoes. How could I report to school without fees or shoes?" Violet explained. "My mother told me to go to classes for tailoring or hairdressing, but I wanted to be a secretary. I was so depressed." Violet thought her schooling was over.

At that time, KGSA didn't have its own toilet, so students walked down the street in small groups during class breaks to Stara, another school down the block. They waited until the headmistress was busy and snuck in to use their toilet. One day, Violet's aunt saw three girls about Violet's age in street clothes crossing the road together.

She asked, "What are you up to? Where are you going?"

The girls said, "We're in a school."

"Which school?"

They pointed at KGSA.

"Why are you not in school uniforms?"

"At our school, you just come as you are."

The girls told her that it was free.

"Lunch and books are provided. We just bring a plate and spoon. If you can, you bring a chair from home."

Violet went to KGSA the next day to register and was accepted right away.

"When I went to class, the girls looked just how they did at home.

You couldn't tell who the teacher was. We sat six girls on each side and a few more on the ends of these long tables. I realized right away how far behind I was." She leaned over during her first class and asked the girl next to her, "What's biology?"

Violet worked hard and caught on fast. She got to school at six in the morning to do her homework because her aunt's house didn't have electricity. Teka recognized Violet's talent and ambition right away and named her prefect. Eventually she became head girl.

"Teachers were busy teaching, so we made sure the students were disciplined. I was strict with them. Some of them went ahead and hated me. Mr. Teka told me to stand strong as head girl. I was good at my job. The school was running very smoothly," Violet said.

Although Violet was excelling at KGSA, it was getting harder for her to stay. Her mother moved in with her and her aunt. Her mother did house work for 1,500 shillings per month, less than twenty U.S. dollars, and rent was 600 shillings, seven U.S. dollars. That didn't leave much money for food. She ate lunch at KGSA, and if there was extra food, she packed a little in a paper bag and brought it home for supper. Her mother said, "Keep on praying, keep on moving. One day God will bless you."

Teka noticed that Violet was often lethargic at school. "Mr. Teka, I feel so hungry. Last night, I didn't have any food. Tonight, I will not have any food."

He took 200 shillings out of his pocket and gave it to her. In Kibera, this could buy Violet a few decent meals.

Violet liked physics so much that she changed her goal from becoming a secretary to becoming a civil engineer—she wanted to be a land surveyor. She also excelled in math and Swahili. Abdul created incentives to keep the girls motivated. He bought gifts like books and rulers for the highest performers in each discipline. He also took Violet and the other prefects on trips outside of Kibera.

"That day, you don't just wash your clothes, you iron them! Then Abdul gave us an allowance for the day. I bought some makeup. You want to look good because you have money. Or on the school's birthday, Abdul brought juice and biscuits to school to celebrate. It is a friendly place. When I was sick, I didn't want to stay home. I wanted to go to school. You are learning. At the same time, you are at home. You feel free. The teachers, when it comes to the matter of learning, are your teachers. When it comes to the matters of home, they are your brothers and sisters."

Violet told Teka about her dreams to go to college and become an engineer. He promised to find her a sponsor that would pay for her to go to college if she graduated with a C+ or higher grade. She set her sights on that goal.

Around the world, for the first time in history, there are more people living in urban areas than rural ones and more people living farther away from where food can be cultivated. Kibera is the biggest slum in Kenya. Its population is growing quickly, but its services are not. People living in Kibera lack access to things like clean water, proper sanitation, adequate healthcare, and excellent schools in part because it is not deemed a legal settlement by the Kenyan government. Kiberans typically make between one and five U.S. dollars per day. Because Kenyan secondary education is not yet free for all children, many in Kibera drop out during primary school to start working. Girls in Kibera feel pressure to get married and start having children as soon as they begin menstruating.

What's happening in Kibera is reflected in slums all over the world. In the developing world, ten thousand girls under the age of fifteen get married every day. Half of the girls in the developing world have children before their eighteenth birthdays. These trends perpetuate extreme poverty. Offering girls access to education helps—every year a girl stays in school, her earning potential goes up 10–20 percent, and a girl who finishes secondary school is six times less likely to become a child bride. Women reinvest 90 percent of their earnings in their own families and communities, so the more women make, the better their communities do.

Educated girls are less likely to contract HIV/AIDS or be

trafficked. Educated girls are more likely to marry later and have fewer children, and those children are more likely to go to school and make more significant contributions to family income. Studies show that educating girls is working as a way to combat poverty, yet education is extremely time-consuming and expensive.

It's easy to build school buildings. It's much harder to build school buildings in a strategic location and to fill those buildings with teachers who get paid a living wage and students who are healthy and supported enough to show up every day to learn. Education is not about school buildings, but about creating caring communities full of people who want more for themselves and the children who come after them. It requires strong community leaders who are willing to holistically invest in young people for decades.

Convincing the community that girls can play soccer was easy for Abdul compared to convincing them that girls deserved to go to secondary school. And once he got the girls in school, he had to support them enough so they could stay. That, he learned quickly, required a generous budget. No tuition came in, which meant finding donations. To retain students like Violet, he needed to provide free tuition, free lunch, and free feminine hygiene supplies. Consistency in the classroom required more than just student attendance. He needed to pay teachers enough for them to show up consistently too. This was no small order. He learned that providing uniforms, supporting the parents, and offering recreational activities also helped. One step at a time, Abdul worked toward building a school that girls not only enrolled in, but graduated from.

Abdul's Telkom salary was not enough to keep the school in the black. With thirty students in second year and twenty-five in first year, they were already outgrowing their new space, and they had twice as many students to feed.

Abdul's charismatic personality and ability to tell engaging, inspiring stories came into play on a daily basis. To gain momentum and build the school the girls needed, he had a lot of persuading to do. He had to persuade parents to trust that sending their girls to secondary school would pay off in the long term. He had to persuade teachers—even Teka—to stay until he could find more solid funding for their salaries. And he had to persuade donors that KGSA was a worthy place to invest in, not just once, but on an annual basis. KGSA's budget grew from $825 in 2006 to $3,575 in 2007. To make up this budget, Abdul first asked Sporting Chance for more financial support. They increased their funding from $625 in 2006 to $1,875 in 2007. He also courted and secured a new partner in Vision Africa. The best way to keep girls in the classroom was to offer free lunch. Abdul needed a large, stable organization to take on the growing food budget. Vision Africa was a faith-based agency out of the United Kingdom that organized soccer tournaments. After KGSA won a Vision Africa tournament, Abdul met with Reverend John and Mrs. Packard. They agreed to fund the food at KGSA, and Abdul and John became close friends. Mrs. Packard, however, was skeptical. Abdul encountered increased resistance from her, sensing that she didn't like that Abdul was Muslim, even though KGSA was not an Islamic school. He started bringing his American MSID volunteer Jamie along with him to the meetings.

Before a meeting with Vision Africa, Teka drew up a food budget to cover breakfast and lunch six days each week. It included a rotating schedule of affordable meals: *githeri*, *chapati* and beans, *ugali*, and *sukuma*. Mrs. Packard slashed line items she thought seemed like luxuries.

"Why should the girls have variety in their food? You are asking for too much. Something is better than nothing," she argued.

"The kids need to eat! This is not extravagant," Jamie countered.

They didn't fund Teka's proposed budget, but with what Vision Africa awarded them, they stretched it far enough to feed not only the teachers and girls, but also many of their younger siblings. Students were trained and given the responsibility of purchasing the food on a weekly basis from Kibera markets. The teachers, students, and parents helped cook the meals. Still, the girls were hungry. Many of the students wandered into Abdul and Zakiya's house to help with chores in hopes of being invited to stay for dinner.

As head girl, Violet helped Abdul see that the next step in KGSA's hierarchy of needs should be offering free menstrual pads.

Without access to feminine hygiene supplies, the girls had to take cloth, fold it, and put it in their underwear. They found it disgusting. Some of the girls lived with uncles and male cousins in one-room homes with no privacy, adding to their embarrassment. Going to an all-girls school helped, but it was still a hygiene problem. Some girls, afraid to go to the chalkboard in case they had bled through their clothes, stayed home from school until their period was over. This is true globally as well—one in ten schoolgirls in Africa misses class or drops out completely due to her period, and substituting less hygienic materials like rags or newspaper for sanitary pads or tampons is not a good or viable option.

When visitors asked Abdul if they could donate anything to the school, he always said, "pens and pads." He stored both in the office for his most vulnerable students. "Then we were proud," Violet said. "At first, we didn't know how to use the pads. The visitors taught us and brought us some panties too, so we could show up to school."

Violet shared the donated pads with her aunt, with whom she was staying while attending KGSA. To make them last longer, she wore one all day long and then used a cloth at night. "In the morning I wake up, shower, and I take another pad. Just like that. Life continues."

Providing menstrual pads was more than a hygiene issue. Second to food, men used pads as a currency in exchange for sex. Boys were willing to help, but for a steep price. Boys have money. Girls need money for food and pads.

"Have sex with me," they would say. "Nothing is for free."

This seemingly casual and widely accepted arrangement between boys with money and girls in need carried sizeable consequences. It took foresight and resolve for girls to resist and find another way. Violet said no, but other KGSA girls said yes. Several students got pregnant. KGSA supported the girls having their children and then coming back to school. Some were brave enough to come back, but others didn't. They got a reputation in the community as a school for girls with kids.

Abdul started getting feminine hygiene pads donated through CARE (Cooperative for Assistance and Relief Everywhere), and the pregnancy rate for KGSA girls dropped almost immediately. Violet agreed: "The pads help so much."

The girls were not the only KGSA community members leaving for financial reasons. Abdul also had trouble retaining teachers, and so Jamie started fundraising for teachers' salaries. They paid the teachers whatever they could each month-—500 shillings, sometimes 1,000 shillings. Teka taught six subjects, so he was the highest-paid teacher at thirty-six U.S. dollars per month. Teachers were willing to teach subjects they didn't know much about so they would get paid more. Subsequently, the girls' performance suffered.

At that point in the school's history, teachers would come just for a chance to teach. Abdul was honest about how little he could pay them. The teachers would agree and say things like, "I also came from the same situation. I would like to help the girls of Kibera."

Then after a few weeks, they tended to leave without a word of warning. It was especially hard to find and retain science teachers and female teachers—because there were fewer of both, the high demand kept them in more formal schools that paid better. With the transient and often untrained faculty, the academic performance of the girls suffered. They were off the streets and fed at KGSA, but very few students were testing well.

Musa, an unlikely hire, provided some stability on the staff. Musa was a devoted Muslim with an erect posture and a squinty smile. His proper façade easily turned into a quick-witted sass and boisterous belly laugh. Musa was born and raised in the Makina neighborhood of Kibera. He grew up without a father, and his mother died when he was in his last year of high school. His uncle took him in, and Musa still lives with him today.

In 2006, after scoring a C– on his secondary exam, Musa started a business selling homemade juice. Mango and passion fruit were his bestsellers. He took orders from schools and businesses and made the juice in his home for pick-up. Teka frequented his juice stand and was impressed with his work ethic and his proper Swahili and English. Teka told Musa about KGSA and invited him to stop by.

"You speak well. If you bring that authority to the classroom, you'll teach well. We need someone to teach Swahili," Teka said.

"I've never taught," Musa replied.

"With that fluency in your language, I think you can."

Musa was skeptical and shy. He didn't know if he could stand up in front of the girls, fairly fresh out of secondary school himself, and find his voice. But when Musa saw the tiny school with two small classes of girls, he decided to try it. He went to other teachers with questions and got suggestions for implementing his syllabus. He went to other schools and talked to teachers about their strategies in the classroom. From day one, he was invested in teaching effectively.

"I knew that in time, this school would be stable and it would be among the best, not just in the slum, but in Kenya. I grew up here, and I see it. The girl child, they discard. They see the boy child as very important and the girls not. Here, it gave me a different perspective. Girls are able to do things if they are given a chance. I'm here completely because of the girls. My heart is telling me that this is the last place I will ever work."

Teka, on the other hand, wasn't so sure. When asked if he enjoyed his work, he surprisingly said, "No, I don't want to be a principal. Actually, I don't want to be a teacher. I want to study commerce. That is my dream. I'm a good teacher, I love it, but I don't want to study it." One day, he heard of a vacancy in a bank. He applied and went to the interview in a T-shirt and jeans only to find everyone else in suits.

"Where are you from?" the interviewer asked.

"Kibera."

"Will you leave Kibera if you get this job?"

"No."

"Why?"

"I want to change the community. I have a dream of starting a bank for Kibera."

Later, he got a message saying that he passed the interview and should go for training. He never expected to be offered the job. Some teachers encouraged him to go, but Abdul asked him not to. He said he would look for more money.

But Teka left.

The job required him to go around to the field and open people's accounts for them. He reported to the office in the morning and told his bank manager that he was going to look for customers. Then he would go back to KGSA and teach.

One day, people from the TV news station KGSB came to interview Teka at KGSA. His bank manager saw the program.

The next day, she asked, "Where else do you work?"

"I don't work anywhere."

"Are you sure?"

"Yeah. Why?"

"I saw you on television."

She said that if her boss knew about his second job, she would be sacked. He had to choose. There was good money at the bank, but Teka's heart was not there. He quit and went back to KGSA.

Teka became invested in his work as KGSA's principal. While Abdul was out networking with foundations and possible donors, Teka took the reins at the school. He began by changing the uniform. Originally, KGSA did not require a uniform, because they were expensive. Many of the KGSA students had stayed out of school for a few years after primary school because they couldn't afford tuition. By the time they got to KGSA, these girls were older, more mature, and easily got mistaken as dropouts around Kibera. This was a problem, Teka explained, because men tried to approach and solicit them.

He saw the uniform as a matter of security. Many of the girls crossed through several neighborhoods on their way to school. They got harassed less when they started to wear a uniform. If a new student got lost on her way, people could look at her KGSA sweater and point her in the right direction, knowing that she had a serious purpose and destination.

Teka and the girls picked out a blue plaid skirt, a navy sweater with the KGSA logo that read "Education is the Key to our Future," white socks with blue stripes, a navy tie with white stripes, and a white blouse. The uniform was expensive—over 500 shillings—so Teka did not require it at first. Some girls arrived at school in uniform; others did not.

People in Nairobi often stereotype the slum (and thus the people living there) as dirty, and the girls worked hard to combat that thinking. Because water is scarce in Kibera, many families ration its use to wash uniforms. School is held Monday through Saturday, and the girls who can afford a uniform can usually afford only one. They wash it when they can, which means a single uniform might be worn for weeks between washings.

When the girls traveled outside of Kibera, Teka did a uniform check before they left. The girls lined up in the courtyard, and he made sure they looked sharp. "We make people from Nairobi think twice because we don't look like we are from a slum. The uniform makes the girls look so smart." The uniforms worked. Once the girls started wearing them, morale went up. They looked like the students they were. They felt official, like they belonged, and they started acting like it.

Similarly, Teka enforced dress codes for the teachers. Knowing they didn't get paid enough to buy a brand new wardrobe, he asked teachers to do their best to look official on Monday through Friday. Saturday was casual day.

Requiring a uniform and providing food and pads aided in rates of attendance. Abdul also began to focus on supporting parents in order to buy the girls more time. Some parents in Kibera simply didn't see daughters as long-term financial assets to the family. It's cheaper to have a daughter marry when she starts menstruating so that she becomes the financial responsibility of her husband—one less school fee to pay and one less mouth to feed. These are not heartless sentiments, but rather cultural norms driven by financial scarcity. Families can't always wait four years while a daughter studies to financially benefit from a job earned with that secondary degree. In the 1960s and '70s, a Kenyan could land a white-collar job with a high school diploma, but the economy has changed a great deal since then. A high school diploma comes with a smaller salary and fewer employment guarantees. Phobian Okodoi, the father of eight children, has four children upcountry and four being educated in Kibera. "I am here educating my children so that they will not have the kind of life I have now," he says. "It's a responsibility of a parent to make sure that his kids go to school and work hard. Parents should check the kids' books and help with homework. We have the responsibility to buy girls sanitary towels. I thank Kibera Girls Soccer as a parent who doesn't have the school fees to educate his daughter."

When Phobian's daughter was in primary, he never thought she would go to secondary school. He had resigned himself to finding her a husband, but Teka persuaded him to support his daughter's education.

Teka told Phobian, "If your girl gets a job that pays well after secondary, she will be the one who will help you. As long as your daughter performs well on her exams, we will take care of her college education."

The best way for Abdul to convince parents to keep their girls in school was to offer them a long-term financial perspective. Soccer continued to be an important part of KGSA, and being part of the team had its own financial benefits. The team got free meals and often won money at tournaments. The girls who played knew they were strong. They felt like agents of their own lives, and in Kenya that is a marketable skill.

But not every student was an athlete. Abdul and Teka established afterschool clubs for the girls who were not in soccer to give them a social outlet and, more important, to equip them with marketable skills so they could find work after graduation.

When Abdul opened KGSA in 2006, he did so in the hope that girls would have a place to come and learn for four years. In his opinion, eighteen was a more appropriate age than fourteen to start work and get married. His first students kept creeping closer to graduation, and Abdul kept wondering what more he could do to set them up for success. Very few of them were performing well enough in class to have hopes of getting college scholarships. With no financial safety net, the students at KGSA would need to find work quickly once they graduated. What was happening in the classroom was better than nothing, but it wasn't relevant enough to prepare the girls to earn substantial wages on the streets of Kibera or Nairobi. Abdul wanted to address the whole person, to develop the potential of the girls in and out of the classroom.

KGSA started a Scouting Club, Journalism Club, Drama Club, and Environmental Club. The clubs were a place to encourage the girls to speak up, take on leadership roles, be curious about the world outside of Kibera, hone business skills, be creative, and gain confidence.

KGSA completed its second school year. Abdul was proud of the steps KGSA had taken to provide food, pads, and clubs for the girls, and he was hopeful that the retention rate would remain high. Sporting Chance financed the construction of a third classroom, and the girls left for holiday. While they were away from school, violence broke out in the slum.

On December 27, 2007, Abdul waited eight hours to vote in the Kenyan presidential race. He voted for Ralia Odinga, and Election Day exit polls showed Odinga ahead, with early projections naming him the winner. Odinga had formerly represented Kibera in Parliament. Hopes were high in Kibera, but cynicism crept in as more and more time passed without an official announcement of the winner.

Eventually, it was announced that the incumbent Mwai Kibaki beat Odinga by 230,000 votes. This was a surprising victory by a surprising margin, even in the eyes of Kibaki supporters. An hour after the announcement, Kibaki was sworn in for his second term at a secret evening ceremony in an undisclosed location, a seemingly hasty move. Kibaki began his second term. Odinga accused Kibaki of electoral fraud, and Odinga supporters threatened to hold a rival swearing-in ceremony.

All nongovernment television channels were shut off. Phone lines went down.

Violence immediately erupted in Kibera. Abdul said, "I saw a man take a stick and start hitting the ground with it over and over again, screaming, 'This is not happening! This is not happening!' A group of young men ran by yelling about their rights. This man with the stick looked up and joined them." Mob mentality ensued. The unofficial plan was for everyone to cause chaos. Kibera residents openly admitted that they wanted to burn down all of Nairobi. The police set up barricades all around the slum in an attempt to contain the anger and violence.

Stuck in Kibera, the crowds started looting. They looted the bars first. Once drunk, they moved on to the stores without security, then the markets. The mob and police alike looted everything they could from Toi Market, the largest market in Kibera. They were Kenyans united in crime, carrying large bags of looted clothes. A day later, when everything was gone, they burned the market down.

Some police and protestors were peaceful at first and even tried to march to Uhuru Park, a site historically used for protesting. But nonviolent tactics didn't last. Kiberans marching toward Uhuru with tree branches, symbolizing their nonviolence, were teargassed by police. The neighborhood of Olympic, one of the major entrances to the slum, became a war zone and was also burned. The president's personal army, the GSU, turned out in full riot gear. They too were sent to Kibera to keep the protestors contained in the slum.

Native Kiberans were scared. It didn't feel right. The mob would come out in the morning as early as six, high and drunk, and attack the police with stones. The police and GSU fought back. And when the police got tired of keeping the protestors at bay, a truck would drive up and shoot into the crowd. Two or three people were killed each day. The crowd would back down and then come back the next day. This went on every day for three weeks. Kibera was on lockdown.

"They started burning churches down systematically," Abdul remembers. "They went into one church, stole everything they could carry, burned it down, and then walked straight to the next church. One at a time. This is not supposed to happen. Church is where you are supposed to seek refuge."

Abdul said that a few people started protesting what they genuinely believed was wrong with the election and then others, angry and tired, erupted and took advantage of the chaos to destroy, loot, vandalize, and steal. It was not one tribal group or another. He could hear only Swahili, not any single tribal tongue, being spoken. This was Kenyans against Kenyans.

One day when the police shot into the crowd, a bullet killed a young girl from Kibera. Within two hours of her death, the women of Kibera organized a protest. Jane Odongo, a local community activist, led a group of women through Kibera. They were joined by hundreds of women along the way, all marching for peace.

Jane spoke of locking her door and hiding with her children while boys threw stones and police threw tear gas outside her home. "The air was horrible. The kids were crying and clinging to me. When Mommy can't protect you, who can protect you? Mommy is stronger than a lion. When Mommy can't do it, now that is a dire situation. Kibera was locked. Nothing was coming in, nothing was going out."

She said, "Both the police and the looters would come by door to door, breaking windows and throwing in tear gas, but the men were not home. The women were. Babies were hungry. Men were frustrated and took it out on their wives. So women suffered doubly. When we walked in protest, women came out barefoot, running and crying. We were crying for the death of the child, yes, but there was more to it. We were crying for our country. Crying of hunger."

By the time the women's march reached the district attorney's office, there were over two hundred women assembled. Jane said, "We made a very powerful press statement that was captured nicely by local media. The death of this girl united us across tribal lines." The women went on to form a group called Kibera Women for Peace and Fairness that continues to meet every week to this day. Their march in 2007 embodied the fatigue and frustration of most Kiberans. When a government is corrupt, it is often the most vulnerable citizens who suffer.

President Kibaki had been equated with corruption for years. Back on December 27, 2002, Mwai Kibaki was voted in as the third president of Kenya. He beat Uhuru Kenyatta, the son of Kenya's first president, Jomo Kenyatta, by a significant margin, thus ending the Kenya African National Union (KANU) rule since independence. At his inauguration, Kibaki promised reform, and said that the government would not be run "on the whims of individuals."

The excitement did not last long. On December 3, before the election, Kibaki was badly injured in a car accident, leaving his colleagues to finish his campaign. Rumors of brain damage, then later a stroke, spread throughout the country. None of them were true, but Kibaki appeared changed. In 2005, he dismissed his entire cabinet and rebuilt it with loyalists.

By the 2007 election, the Kenyan people were disappointed in Kibaki, yet he announced he would run again against Ralia Odinga, one of the men he dismissed in 2005. Odinga had the overwhelming backing of the people in Kibera. If elected, he'd be the first president from the majority tribe in Kibera, the Luo. Odinga raised the profile of Nubians in particular and all Kiberans in general. His father Oginda Odinga was a major player in creating the multiparty system in the late 1980s in opposition to the Moi regime. The Odinga name, then, brought with it history and expectations.

The Nubians have always been the numerical minority in Kenya, so they have a history of banding together to help each other out. Makina, a Nubian-networked neighborhood in Kibera, stayed relatively safe during the postelection violence. Abdul said, "We would walk around in large groups at the beginning and tell the people that no looting was going to happen in our neighborhood. We had connections that helped us get food in from the outside. We managed okay. The KGSA girls in other neighborhoods were not so lucky."

Jamiah was a KGSA student who lived close to the railway line, one hot spot of violence between the Kiberans and the police. The railway line marked the farthest point where the police came in and the farthest point where the Kiberans went out. One day, Jamiah saw a group of young men running by her house toward the railway line to start harassing the police. Knowing that their running meant violence was soon to follow, she hurried outside to tell her three younger siblings to get inside to be safe.

"The men on the road were shouting bad names at the police," Jamiah remembered. "They accused the police of coming to take our properties." More people ran by her house to join the crowd, while others around her compound started running for safety. "I heard a gunshot and fell to the ground. I didn't feel pain at first, but I felt something flowing. I saw blood. It was dark. Then I heard my neighbor screaming, 'She's been shot! She's been shot!' That was the last thing I heard."

The bullet hit Jamiah in the right thigh as she was running to get inside her house. Her neighbor carried her inside and wrapped her leg to slow the bleeding. Her mother took her to a clinic in Kibera and then to a hospital for an operation to remove the bullet.

"I was admitted for three days. It took a month to heal. I couldn't stand on my own. It still hurts when it's cold out or when I stand for too long or have to walk a long distance." She was in her last year of primary school at the time.

There are two major bus companies in Nairobi. City Hoppa, the green buses, are run by Kikuyus and had posters up before the election promoting Kibaki. Green buses were burned during the postelection violence, and they still, ten years later, refuse to enter Kibera. One day during the riots, there was a lot of shooting, and the police killed eight people. The protestors were so angry, they managed to lift up the railway line running through Kibera while the police stood by and watched.

There were three phases of police lockdown, and during each phase, the KGSA girls ran out of food. They asked Abdul for help. He connected with a friend, a policeman, to get in and out of the slum

for work. While he was out, he also met with Jamie. He told her what
was happening on the inside, and she gave him money that she had
raised from the United States. They were going to use the money to
buy desks and chairs for the new classroom, but Abdul used it for food
to feed the girls.

"It got tough because my neighbors started coming for my help
too. Everyone was hungry and scared. Kibera was quarantined."
Abdul remembered, "I met up with Jamie one day a few weeks into
the fighting to get more food. Her neighbors were grilling meat for
dinner. The smell was amazing. People in Kibera were starving and
being shot at and dying, and this family was feasting on meat peace-
fully in the safety of their home. These two different worlds are so
close to each other. I was one of the few during that time who got
out of the chaos in Kibera and saw how others were living. The only
things the rich missed were their nannies. They had to stay at home
with their kids. They had to cook their own food because their cooks
were stuck in Kibera."

One day when Abdul was returning to Kibera, he saw a wall of
plainclothes police officers standing by their cars watching the fighting.
There were maybe twelve of them, all heavily armed. He heard one
man say to another, "Who owns Kibera anyway? Let's burn it down.
Let's just kill them all."

The police were exhausted, and they slipped into more and more
brutal means of keeping peace. The tear gas eventually got so bad that
kids in the border neighborhoods got sick. Large trucks would come
by to spray water on the protestors. To this day, the sight of flatbed
trucks still triggers bad memories for Abdul.

Internationally, people understood the postelection violence as
tribal—the tribes of the two candidates turning against each other.
Kibaki is Kikuyu, and other tribes believed the election was a fraud-
ulent attempt to keep power within the large Kikuyu tribe. Most
people in Kibera will tell you the violence was about poverty. It was
the people of Kibera, desperate for change, fighting for the government to take notice of their living situation. People who were tired

of being poor fought the police. No one particular person or force or threat stopped the postelection violence—the people just got tired of fighting. The protestors met and agreed to approach the police. They said, "Get the police out of here and we'll stop fighting." So the police left. Then those same people who pulled up the railway line worked to replace it.

KGSA was closed for the holiday when the violence in Kibera started. Some of the girls were back in the upcountry with family, while others ventured out to get food from Abdul. When Jamie and Abdul were working to open the new school, they splurged and bought desks and beautiful red-and-blue padded folding chairs to encourage the girls and make the new building feel more like home. They were the first proper desks and chairs the school had acquired. Before that, they had used butcher-block tables and rented chairs. Abdul had to beg the workers to come into Kibera to deliver the items and had to personally guarantee their safety.

The school was built with mud, so when the looting started, someone dug a hole in the foundation and stole a few of the chairs for his family. There was so much chaos that Kiberans took advantage of their own neighbors and turned on each other. A few windows were broken in the school, but that and the stolen chairs were the only damages sustained during the postelection violence.

The violence, theft, vandalism, property loss, and looting lasted two months across the country. An estimated 500,000 people were forced to leave their homes. Large numbers of killings and sexual assaults were reported during that time. Police killed protestors. Violence was caught on television, and, after those scenes aired, the reaction was more violence.

Meanwhile, several cabinet members refused to recognize Kibaki as president. The 2007 election was reviewed by the Independent Review Commission, which reported such wide-scale corruption in every region with every candidate that it was impossible to report who really won. They found bribery, vote buying, intimidation, and ballot stuffing on all sides of the election, although admittedly more so on the side of Kibaki, who remained president and elected Odinga as prime minister. The government kept all schools closed throughout Kenya until the violence subsided. It was a great homecoming at KGSA when school was called back in session for the New Year, now with three grades instead of two. The number of students grew in all three grades because there was more need. Many families lost jobs, businesses, and property during the burning and looting and could no longer pay tuition. Abdul had seen many of the older girls who came by looking for food, but he was happy to see more of the girls show up when school resumed.

"We lost a lot of girls," Abdul said. "Many had fled at the beginning of the violence and did not come back. We went looking for them all because they were family. Eventually, some of the girls would reappear years later, playing for different soccer teams, but some we never saw again. We lost Christine, Agnes's niece, during the violence. She went to the rural area and never came back. We heard later that she got pregnant and was too embarrassed to return. She was such a good student, so focused. It was hard to lose her."

During the violence, Christine and Agnes were displaced to a slum called Satellite. Agnes came back, but Christine moved to a different slum, got pregnant, and Jamie and Abdul never found her. They don't know if she was raped, had sex because she was desperate for food, or needed comfort from a boyfriend. She had a baby boy and never returned to Kibera.

"KGSA doesn't turn girls away, and we wanted her to come back," Jamie said. "Abdul tried to track her down. She didn't have a phone. We tried to communicate through a messenger, but she lived eight hours away. It was not practical to just go wandering into a village to look for a girl. She had a little boy, and she didn't finish school. Agnes gave me a picture of her, and I have it on my fridge. She said to me, 'When you go home, remember me. Remember we are strong.'"

The postelection violence changed people. They had hope but they were left to deal with both electoral fraud and the violence that ensued after. They didn't want to fight their neighbors anymore. They don't hope as much now. The polls show that the majority of Kenyans don't trust their president. And in the following election, eighteen million voters were expected to show up but only twelve million did.

Abdul voted in 2012. He voted for Odinga again but doesn't believe it was a fair election. "He got most of the votes in Kibera again. He got most of the votes in Kenya, but he didn't win. There is apathy around politics now. Kiberans don't want to talk about it; they just want to work." People were holding their collective breath, waiting for violence to break out again after the 2012 election results were announced, and there was a collective sigh of relief when nothing happened. They were still so tired from the last election.

The nature of violence changed too. Before 2007, it was more organized, with more consistent and predictable rules. There was a code of honor: Gangs didn't attack local Kiberans, but instead attacked the middle-class neighborhoods surrounding Kibera. It was considered shameful to steal from people who had next to nothing. Now, there are fewer neighborhoods that are safe. There are muggings in broad daylight. People who have lived in Kibera their whole lives feel unsafe. The police will do nothing in Kibera.

Jamiah said, "Maybe some of the police are heartless. Not all of them are around to keep us safe. We are in charge of our own justice, and we are still hungry."

THE PROBLEMS OF THE URBAN POOR
ARE EVERYBODY'S PROBLEMS

2008

If you want to go fast, go alone; if you want to go far, go together.

—AFRICAN PROVERB

When Asha's father Jaffar was ten, his grandmother made him promise to name his first daughter after her. He lived up to his promise. Asha's great-grandmother was a stern, independent woman who never had a husband. She didn't give into societal pressure to marry, and instead raised her children and grandchildren on her own. Asha's father tells her she looks like her great-grandmother. "I even share some of her mannerisms and habits," Asha said. "Like I caught her spirit; I am proud to be her namesake."

Asha's mother Zubeda was born in Uganda, the granddaughter of a member of Parliament. At age ten, she was forced to come to Kenya as a refugee during the Idi Amin era. Zubeda's mother, Khadijah, was very educated but lost all her documents in the war and could not prove her status in Kenya. They lived in a tent provided by the UN in a refugee camp on the border of Uganda and Kenya for a few years where Khadijah taught her daughter Zubeda to plait hair and cook samosas to make money. Zubeda stopped going to school in the eighth grade. Khadijah opened a restaurant while her husband worked as a driver for the Saudi Arabian embassy.

They sent Zubeda to Kibera to stay with relatives. There, she met Jaffar and has stayed with him ever since. She never went back to school, but Asha remembers thinking that her mother was very smart because she spoke English.

Asha asked, "Why did you leave school in the eighth grade?"

Zubeda said, "I don't like talking about my past. Maybe you will look down on me because I am not educated."

The war was hard on Asha's mother. Zubeda said the sounds of bombs and gunshots were still in her head thirty years later. Asha worried about her.

"The life she lived, I understand," Asha said. "She didn't go to school. She was so young when she married my father and had me. I think I trapped her in a life she didn't want."

Asha's family, like many families in Kibera, did not have a toilet. Because Kibera is not recognized by the government as an official city, no public funds go toward sanitation, and few individuals can afford to build their own toilet. It's an issue of privacy, health, and dignity. Asha and her siblings urinated on small pieces of used polythene and threw them out on the terrace. They defecated into small plastic bags and threw them on the ground. The nearest toilet they could use was a ten-minute walk from the house and cost five shillings per use. The kids learned to relieve themselves just about anywhere they could, leaving an environment and a stench that neighbors with toilets complained about.

Asha shared a mattress with her sister Sherifa on the floor. When it rained, water came through the roof into their room. They'd fight over their shared blanket and cry from the cold.

There were stretches when Asha's family didn't have sufficient water. Asha got up at five, sometimes four when it was very scarce, to go find water. And that water needed to be boiled to be safe to drink.

Her stomach ached from the poor water and hunger. They ate boiled maize, which didn't suffice. When her siblings complained of hunger, she crept with them over to their neighbor's trash bin to pull out pieces of fruit. They sifted through the trash for the fruit, shook it off, and sucked on the remaining strings of fiber. It was the same bin he threw his feces in. One day, the neighbor asked Asha's mother why his trash bin seemed emptier every day.

"Maybe it's the dogs," Zubeda said.

When she realized it was her children, she beat them for their bad behavior.

"We couldn't help it," Asha said. "We were hungry."

Years later, Asha heard that her neighbor was HIV positive. She didn't know much about the disease and worried that she could have contracted HIV by eating fruit with his saliva and feces on it. She was skinny and getting skinnier from lack of nutrition, having only black tea for breakfast and boiled maize for dinner, no meat and seldom any milk. She was tested for HIV at school and was convinced she would test positive. When it came back negative, she danced around the room in relief.

Jaffar worked hard to maintain several rental properties for profit, and over the years, he built a toilet and beds and expanded the house. Asha worried though, because she thought the stress of providing for his wife and six children would one day be too much.

She heard him say, "I just want to leave you people and go away because things are getting hard for me."

So on nights when it reached midnight and he didn't show up, she told her siblings, "Maybe he left us."

But he didn't.

As the oldest, Asha cared for her five younger siblings while her parents worked. At night, the kids would call for Asha, not their mother, to come and comfort them. At age ten, she was changing diapers, feeding babies, and kissing scraped knees. She grew up quickly. When her mother came home from work, if anything seemed amiss in the house, she beat Asha. Asha showed her swollen hands to her father when he came home from work. "Is she really my mother?" Asha asked him.

She garnered her strength, proud that she could withstand being beaten without crying. At night, she asked God, "If you love your children, why do you let me suffer? If I'm supposed to love my parents, why doesn't my mother love me back?"

One evening, before her father came home from work, her baby sister started fussing while her mother was making dinner. Asha couldn't get her sister to calm down, and her mother snapped. Zubeda grabbed Asha by the arm and held her hand over the kerosene lamp until it burned. Instead of screaming in pain, Asha went straight to her room and skipped dinner out of sheer anger. The next morning, she showed her father her burned hand.

"Look what mother did to me," she said. Then she left for school.

That same day, Jaffar took her out of class at school. "Where are we going?" she asked.

"Your aunt's house," he replied.

She lived with Zalikah, her aunt, for two years. Life was difficult there as well. Her three cousins teased her for being beaten and burned. One of Asha's jobs was fetching charcoal for the *jiko*. She came back with the charcoal and tried to leave to shower and do her homework.

Her cousin refused to light the *jiko,* saying, "I cannot touch charcoal. These are things you are used to doing. You are black like charcoal, so it won't matter."

This wasn't the first time she had been compared to charcoal. She was born in Kenya, but her Nubian great-grandparents came from Southern Sudan. Asha's skin was very dark. In Kibera, the culture says the lighter the skin the better. In class at school, her teacher asked the class for examples of similes.

One student offered, "As dark as coal."

Another added, "As dark as Asha."

Lighter-skinned girls refused to sit by her. Boys called her a black monkey. For as long as she could remember, Asha associated her dark skin with dirtiness. She grew up hating her color.

Asha's mother assumed that her kids would live a life similar to hers: go to school through primary, drop out, live in Kibera, and raise families. Her grandmother also assumed this was the plan for Asha. Zubeda and Khadijah believed that as soon as a girl started menstruating, she was ready to behave like a woman, get married, and start having babies. Asha's Islamic school teacher told her that girls have to start taking life seriously when they start menstruating. They have to start behaving in a way worthy of being a man's wife. They have to learn how to cook, care for babies, clean, and be responsible. In the Nubian culture, it's common for parents to sell their daughters off at a young age. A man will see a girl he likes and approach the parents of the girl with interest. When the girl starts menstruating, the parents will go to the family of the man and arrange the marriage. There are more and more women marrying by choice, but it is more difficult if the girl is poor.

Asha wanted more. "Some girls start menstruating at age nine. That is no time to be a wife!" She was determined to shock her whole community someday by announcing, "I am going to college." But there was a distinct pressure starting when a girl began menses. It became a fight to stay in school.

Asha felt lucky that she didn't start her period until her second year at KGSA. But still, when it happened, she did not feel ready to be married. She wanted to study. "Maybe if my mother were nice I wouldn't know how to fight. But I have fight in me."

On her first day at KGSA, Asha realized she had bought the wrong uniform tie. Her tie matched the plaid of the skirt, but the other girls had navy ties with white stripes. She also brought a bright yellow desk. Some girls poked fun at her, and others commented on how tall she was. But she was undeterred. When teachers asked her to introduce herself to the class, she did so in a loud, clear voice.

"Do you want to be here to continue your education or were you forced?" they asked.

"I want to come. It was my will to come to school."

Many girls, when they join KGSA as first-year students, are timid and insecure. They haven't found their voices yet. Asha was not like most girls. Teka remembered her raising her hand to speak repeatedly on her first day. When there was an opportunity to send some students to an HIV/AIDS awareness event in Machakos, Teka sent Asha with some third-year students.

"Take Asha," he said. "She knows how to speak her mind."

It was her first time out of Nairobi. She met girls from schools outside of Kibera and thought, "I want to talk like those girls."

Meeting girls from bigger schools who had lived very different lives than Asha inspired her. The next day at KGSA, she asked Teka if she could join the Journalism Club.

"Yes, grab a seat. Write about everything."

Asha started KGSA in 2008, right after the postelection violence. During the violence, the government closed all the schools in Kenya for three weeks, so the 2008 school year started late. When school reconvened, there were twenty-five girls in third year, twenty-five in second year, and thirty in first year. The school lost some students who had been displaced, but the violence also created more need in Kibera. Some families who could afford secondary tuition before the violence were now no longer able to.

With KGSA adding one more class each year, the budget swelled with more free lunches to serve, more free menstrual pads to distribute, and more teachers to pay. Sporting Chance, Vision Africa, and the MSID students in the United States paid for food and construction for the new school building on Konga's land, but KGSA needed major funding partners. In 2008, they found those partners. PADEM, or Programmes d'Aide et de Développement destinés aux Enfants du Monde, is a French nongovernmental organization working to improve the quality of life for children by partnering with local civic groups in developing countries. In 2007, KGSA had raised $3,575. Because of a $22,000 grant from PADEM, in 2008, the budget was $26,500.

PADEM found KGSA through a film featuring Abdul. Abdul

knew the girls' lives were compelling, and some of the girls were eager to have their stories told. Abdul understood that to get money into Kibera, he had to get information about their standard of living out of the slum. Film was an effective way to show people around the world how they lived.

One day, Abdul's friend called him and said, "I met these freelance film guys who are working for the UN making documentaries. You have to come meet them. Now."

Abdul agreed and met up with them. He told them the story of KGSA.

David Gough, the lead filmmaker, was immediately interested. He had been in Kibera for a while, but he hadn't yet found a local charismatic storyteller like Abdul. David loved both Abdul and the concept of the school. KGSA was his missing puzzle piece.

Abdul knew enough about the UN to know that this was not an opportunity to pass up. When David Gough asked to feature KGSA in his film about Kibera, Abdul agreed.

Hoping this would be KGSA's first big break in the new location, Abdul put in sixteen hours on tape. He and David became fast friends. David trained him to be more effective on camera, considering eye contact, volume, and enunciation. It still pays off to this day. As of the publication of this book, KGSA has been featured in eight films over seven years.

The filmmakers don't give money directly to the featured subjects. The UN shows the documentaries in diplomatic circles all over the world, and funding may come from the film's networking capabilities. The film team launched *Slum Survivors* at the UN-IRIN (United Nations Integrated Regional Information Networks) offices at Gigiri in Nairobi. Abdul was invited to attend. At that point, Abdul had not yet seen the film and had no idea what to expect.

It was exciting to see so many viewers and so much buzz about a film he'd appeared in. After segments on a mother with HIV, a man who had turned away from a gang life full of drugs, stealing, and violence, and a man who emptied latrines to provide for his family,

Abdul appeared onscreen. There he was, in a soccer jersey and jeans, sitting by a barbed-wire fence with a trash-filled dirt road behind him, explaining his dream.

"I saw that there was no gender equity between the girl child and the boy child here in Kibera," he said to the camera. "At that small level that I was at, I thought we should start making these girls do things that these men can do, and they can do it fairly better. So we started a girls' soccer team."

He explained how his twelve- and thirteen-year-old players never went to secondary school. Some started getting pregnant, so he opened the school. There was footage of a new classroom being built, and he spoke about how badly he felt when he couldn't pay the teachers. The film cut to Christina, a KGSA student, brushing her teeth as the narrator explained how she cared for her five siblings and chose to attend KGSA against her father's will.

"Staying at Abdul's school, even though it is free, is a constant battle," the narrator said. She pointed out that Abdul could use the land for something that made him money, but he didn't. She quoted him, adding, "The problems of the urban poor, he says, are everybody's problems."

As Abdul climbed onto a train to head out of Kibera to his job, his voice-over said, "Education is only replacing an empty mind with an open mind."

The viewers saw Abdul, looking out of the train window toward the slum. "If there was an equitable distribution of resources all over the world, chances are there would be a more peaceful world."

David invited Abdul to address the crowd. The feedback on the film was positive. David told Abdul that they distributed 8,000 copies of the film in hopes of spreading interest and concern to people around the world.

The making and launch of *Slum Survivors* was a turning point for Abdul. Kibera was not on the map, literally or figuratively, but now his dream of letting the world know that Kibera existed was coming true.

After it aired and started circulating in Europe, David wrote Abdul and said that representatives from a French organization had liked the film and had asked him for Abdul's contact information. Shortly after, Abdul received an email from a woman named Magali Getrey. She represented PADEM, and she told Abdul she was coming to Kenya to see the school.

"Okay, now this is serious," Abdul said aloud to his computer screen.

Magali and her husband came to see KGSA. They were a hit, taking the whole student body out to dinner and dancing. When they left, she told Abdul, "Keep your fingers crossed on July 13th. That is the day of a decisive meeting. I will be in touch."

After the meeting, Magali wrote Abdul and said, "Your program has gone through. We found you funding in France. We will send you 50,000 euros over three years. What are your priorities?"

The school had run for two years on less than $5,000. Abdul had been waiting for this day. He knew what the next step needed to be.

"I want to build. I want to expand the school."

"Okay, can you get a contractor?"

"No, I want the people of Kibera to build this school."

Abdul knew that if Kiberans built the school, a piece of them would remain with KGSA. He wanted the Kiberans to feel like they owned the school. They needed to keep growing. With PADEM's money, KGSA started the final construction phase of a third classroom. The school logo, matching the emblem on the uniform sweaters, was painted on the wall. Desks were purchased for the entire third-year classroom.

Every quarter, Abdul wrote a report to PADEM, attached receipts, and sent them by post. And every quarter, PADEM sent another one-fourth of the annual funds promised. For the first time in the school's history, Abdul breathed easier and looked around at what the school needed beyond teachers, food, menstrual pads, and classrooms.

Abdul saw the effects of the postelection violence in the girls at school. Jamiah had a low KCPE score on the national exam in primary, in part because she missed three weeks of school after being shot. KGSA accepted Jamiah in spite of her low test scores, but she continued to struggle. She said she worried about who would keep her siblings safe while she was in class.

"Maybe if I wasn't there to tell them to get inside, it would be them and not me getting shot." Girls just started crying in class. Students who were usually attentive fell asleep. Abdul named a couch in the library "the Chill-Out Zone" and told teachers to allow girls to take a break from school to relax.

The girls were coming to school under a lot of pressure. The global financial crash of 2008 hit Kenya, and specifically Kibera, hard. Food prices rose globally. Kiberans started buying bread by the slice, not the loaf. The government was slow to subsidize milk and maize.

Abdul and Teka considered the broader factors limiting the girls' academic performance. If they wanted KGSA to thrive instead of just survive, Abdul and Teka decided they had to address the parents. The better the parents were doing, the better the girls would be doing. They expanded the circle of support, redefining who belonged to and benefited from KGSA.

Abdul started visiting KGSA families to observe how they were living. Many had lost property and businesses from looting. None of them could afford enough food. All of them were scared. Some parents unleashed their anger on their children. KGSA offered one free meal a day, and that was all many of the girls were eating. Abdul and Teka knew they had to financially support the parents so the girls could stay in school instead of getting married or starting to work.

"There was again more pressure on the girls to earn money and drop out of school. We couldn't have that. We needed to relieve the pressure at home so the girls could learn," Abdul said.

"So I talked to PADEM, and they visited the girls in their homes too. The students suggested that if the parents were given some money to start a business, they could support the kids to work hard in school. PADEM put in 2,000 euros, close to U.S. $3,000 at the time, for us to start a microfinance program. We trained the parents and gave them a bit of money to get going again. And you know what? It worked.

The kids stopped needing the Chill-Out Zone. They came to school ready to learn."

There were one hundred people who came to the first microfinance meeting, ninety of whom were women. KGSA hired Faridah, the Girls Soccer in Kibera player, to help run the microfinance program. "My job is walking to see the businesses. I need to know where my clients live and what kind of business they do," she said. "It's hard to be an orphan and a single mother—it can get lonely. I'm much better off now that I have to go see people for my job."

Faridah's mother was sick for seven years and couldn't work before she died. Faridah tells the KGSA parents her mother's story to encourage them to be grateful to have work. Parents can ask for 5,000-, 10,000-, or 15,000- shilling loans, around U.S. $60, $120, or $175, according to the size of their business. The groups met weekly and were trained in budgeting and saving. It was a place to bring concerns, both personal and professional.

"We share as a family," Faridah said. "The parents are part of KGSA. They share, and we find solutions."

Part of the savings went into a social fund to help the groups pay for unexpected life expenses like medical bills. At the end of the year, the rest of the savings was given back to them. KGSA gave small loans from the savings. If a parent took 1,000 shillings, about twelve U.S. dollars, she came back with 200 shillings, or two U.S. dollars, in interest. The interest was distributed to the parents at the end of the year.

"We also have a merry-go-round. Every meeting they come with 100 shillings. When it is your turn, the money is given to you."

The microfinance program for the KGSA parents is so essential because, as Teka said, "People don't have access to banking services here in Kibera. No one from the outside trusts us or wants to deal with such small sums of money. Ultimately, my dream is to start a bank in Kibera for Kiberans. That is why I want to go to university for finance and commerce. Here, for a parent to be given a loan, she needs to have security. We rely on social security in our microfinance program. We give the loan to the whole group, and the whole group needs to make sure that the loans are paid back."

Tailoring businesses seem to be doing well, as are food shops. In Kibera, the women like putting on good clothes and looking sharp, and people have to eat. Faridah said the biggest challenge was when parents had to take money away from their business for family expenses. It was a big change for some of the mothers in the program to wait and trust that the capital would turn into profit. Saving is scary if one has never done it.

Families also had to adjust to having women running businesses. "They used to be dependent on their husbands. The first meeting, I was calling the roster, and there was one parent missing. 'Do you know where this person is?'"

"No," the others said.

"The next meeting, I called the roster again, and she was missing again. Now I was forced to call her. Why are you not coming to the meetings?" She told me she was not feeling well.

"Then the third meeting, I called the roster again, and she was not there. So I had to go see her. She was being beaten by her husband. That's why she wasn't coming. Her husband didn't want her to go out of the house and start a business. She was supposed to stay home. I told the group, and we decided to pay her a visit. We went and her husband was there. We talked to him and changed his mind. Now he lets her come to the meetings. At times, the husbands think the wives are going to see other men. There's a lot of insecurity as the women are learning business."

There were fathers in the group as well. Phobian Odinga took his 10,000-shilling loan and started buying and selling eggs. He made bread for people in the morning and sold cigarettes in the after-noon. In the evening, he sold kale and tomatoes. "With the profit I get from the small business, I buy books for my children. I had a worn shoe, and now thanks to the microfinance, I'm able to buy a new shoe and sustain myself and life," he said. "I was able to start a worthy life. They visit me at my house and track my well-being.

This is a school, and yet they care that my business is going well too."
Teka said, "We had only 100,000 shillings to give from the
PADEM grant. It could not be enough to help everyone. But the ones
who stayed are taking it very seriously. The difference was felt almost
immediately." KGSA was becoming more than a school.

Jamiah said that as a third-year student she was concentrating better
in school. She wanted to do better on her KCSE than on her KCPE. "I
try to forget," she said. "Life should begin."

Faridah was not the only Girls Soccer in Kibera player hired at KGSA
in 2008. Abdul got Claris to come back too. Claris loved her boarding
school experience in Kisumu and fell in love with math while she was
there. In math class, after her teacher did an example on the board,
Claris would ask to do the next one. At the board, she imagined being
a teacher someday.

Claris was sure she was university material, but she earned only a
C+ on her KCSE exam. With a C+, she'd have to pay tuition. With
no hope for a college scholarship, she moved back into her mother's
home after graduation. While she had been away, some of her siblings
had gotten into prostitution or ended up on the streets. They came
back sick, or with children of their own. Without the geographical
distance and no further studies to keep her busy, she started worrying.
She had the most education, and her siblings were looking to her for
support.

She stayed up at night wondering, "How will my family survive?"

When Claris's boarding school was on holiday break, she'd visit
Abdul and the girls at KGSA. She volunteered in the classroom,
mentored the new goalies, and helped to organize soccer matches.

When she graduated, she went to Abdul at KGSA and said, "I can
teach math and geography. The girls know me. They know where I
come from. I can reach them."

"Definitely," he said. "But you can't teach in that track suit."

He gave her some money and told her to buy clothes that would
help her feel like a teacher. Her professional wardrobe gave her confi-

dence to believe that she could deliver. She taught classes at KGSA during the day, became a soccer official, and trained soccer goalies in Kibera in the evening. With an income, the first thing she did was buy furniture. She bought a few chairs and new beds for her mother's house. One by one, her siblings moved back in.

She proudly told her students that on her teaching salary at KGSA, she was supporting her mother and fourteen siblings.

"I told them that I'm holding my family together. I teach them math, but I also show them that staying in school pays off. They too will be able some day to buy furniture for their families and make their homes beautiful."

After she provided some financial stability for her family, she decided to pay her own tuition. She couldn't afford university, but she started to take night classes at Kenya Institute of Management, working toward a certificate in business management. That also did some effective modeling for her students. They were proud that their math and geography teacher, Ms. Claris, who grew up in Kibera, was reaching beyond the secondary level for more education. Claris established herself and continues to be a stable female force at KGSA. Like Teka and Musa, she has stayed and grown tremendously as a teacher during her tenure. Her consistent presence is even more valuable, considering that it is harder to retain female teachers than male.

Another important addition to the KGSA faculty in 2008 was Josephat, Linet's brother. Linet's mother got sick with malaria while Linet was in third year. She started going to school without food at home more and more often because Alice was too sick to work and purchase food. To support her mother, Linet started doing laundry for small sums of money.

She asked neighbors, "Do you have anything else for me to wash so we can eat?"

At home, Alice shivered terribly while her body temperature continued to rise. She worried aloud to Linet: "When I die, I am going to leave you in a bad state."

Linet and Josephat were with Alice in her upcountry home when she died. With over a year of school left, Linet didn't see how she could continue to attend KGSA and make enough money to survive.

"Come back to Nairobi," Teka told her. "You have to finish school." Abdul hired Josephat as a teacher at KGSA so he could support Linet while she studied. He was not trained to be a teacher, but the students liked him, and they learned.

Abdul had found people like Claris, Faridah, and Josephat who needed the school as much as the school needed them. Instead of finding trained teachers in Nairobi, he preferred the teachers who understood what the girls and parents at KGSA were dealing with outside the classroom. They had instant rapport. It was these teachers who, despite the low pay, stayed year after year, offering increased stability to the girls. The staff grew from eight to thirteen in 2008. Teacher salaries were raised to 4,000 shillings a month, close to fifty U.S. dollars, in hopes of retaining them—still only one-third of the 12,000-shilling salary of a teacher in a government-run school. With the teachers and the parents doing well, the girls started to do better too.

Two American women supported the staff of locals that year. The MSID volunteer in 2008 was Aisling Culhane, a student from the University of Wisconsin at Madison who loved soccer and photography. "Kenya was overwhelming at first. It's so colorful, loud, dirty, and smelly. KGSA was a single one-story building and one two-story building with three very small, crowded classrooms. Then they had the teacher's lounge—a room with one table in it—the beginnings of a computer lab, and one latrine."

Teka asked Aisling to help with the Journalism Club. "It was hard to get girls to stay after school. They had a very long day, and many girls played soccer. We did writing workshops and photography one day a week. There were only a few computers in the teacher's lounge collecting dust because there was rarely electricity and never Internet access and no access to cameras."

She assisted teachers, helped grade papers, made lunch, and supervised tests. When she wasn't needed on testing days, she babysat the kids next door to the school so their mother could do laundry. She remembered the girls struggling in the classroom, scoring low on tests—in part because they were tested in English, a language many of the girls hadn't mastered. One day, she went with Musa to his house to pick something up, and seeing his small ten-by-twelve home in the slum made her fully realize that the KGSA teachers were barely compensated for their work.

The other American woman, Anne Baldwin, first came to Kenya with a study-abroad trip through Kalamazoo College in 2008. She was connected with Carolina for Kibera (CFK), and her first task was to work at a donation tent in the middle of Kibera. CFK decided to host a five-kilometer race and give out donated shoes to the runners as prizes at the end.

Anne was embarrassed to be working at an event that was so poorly planned by outsiders. "They didn't provide water, food, or childcare. So women were running the five-K without shoes, holding babies. There were more runners than shoes, so it ended in a riot— women crowding the tent and ripping shoes away from one another and fighting over T-shirts. It was awful."

After the five-K, Anne decided that CFK might not be a good fit. She did an Internet search for other organizations and found KGSA.

She called Abdul and he said, "Great! Come to our soccer game this weekend!"

After the soccer game, Abdul took Anne on a tour of Kibera and to see the school. Anne remembered it taking hours because of how often Abdul was enthusiastically greeted and pulled aside by people— adults and kids alike—to talk. Most conversations ended with Abdul handing the person a few shillings. She saw how generous he was and knew she wanted to be with him every step of the way.

Anne was welcomed aboard, and she started teaching right away. She wrote her research paper for her study-abroad program about the connection between soccer and science. "The girls at KGSA had gotten so good at soccer and remembered the days when they weren't allowed to play. They thought, 'Girls can't play soccer? We'll show you!' But they actually believed that girls can't do science."

Anne taught physics at KGSA and at first it was hard. The girls laughed at her American accent and couldn't understand her phrasing. English in Kenya is spoken differently, and for most girls, it was their third language. One girl would eventually understand Anne and translate her words for the class. With time, Anne adjusted and improved. She talked about how hard it was to come up with real-world examples to explain concepts to girls in a slum.

"How do you teach water pressure to a girl in Kibera? The book talks about the pressure you feel at the bottom of a pool. They don't have a pool. Or static electricity: The book explains when you walk on carpet in socks and your hair stands on end. OK, for one, that's not Kenyan hair. And they don't have carpets or socks!

"I wanted them to know that science is not only fun, but useful. I think math and science and computer science will get you a job. Teaching applied and practical science would put people in a slum ahead of people in a big public school teaching cut-and-dry textbook science. Without needing to get into a college program, girls could be mechanics or electricians and make good money.

"In 2008," she said, "the school was still rough-and-tumble, outside the lines, informal and energetic. It was Abdul's baby, still very much in formation. It was exciting to be a part of it."

Anne returned from her six months in Kenya knowing that she wanted to go back, and she found a way in 2010.

Claris was correcting math papers in the office with Teka when a girl walked in holding a man's hand.

The man said, "This is my daughter. She wants to start school. Can you take her?"

"Are you ready for school?" Claris asked the girl.

"Of course I'm ready! I've been struggling to get to school."

Teka looked at her intently and said, "Then at 10:00 a.m. be here with your chair, a plate, a spoon, and a pen to write."

"How much do I pay?" she asked.

"You pay zero."

She smiled at them both before darting out of the room. The girl went home, bathed, tore out the pages in her notebook that had writing on them, and put the blank pages in a bag. She didn't have chairs at home, only stools, so her father borrowed a chair from his workplace for her to bring. She got back to school by ten and was directed to Claris's math room. The girls in the class were bent over their desks, taking a test.

"You came back," Claris smiled. "What's your name?"

"Lynn."

Claris handed Lynn a math book and said, "You're behind. You have to take the exams the girls are taking right now. Read about decimals until you understand everything. Start cramming."

Lynn read about decimals and closed her book. Claris handed her the test. She did all the calculations and handed it back to her new teacher.

Over the next few days, each teacher did with Lynn what Claris had done. They gave her the book, showed her the section, asked her to cram, and gave her the exam her classmates were taking.

In between tests, barely believing she was in school, Lynn looked around and saw that she was one of the only students not in uniform. She asked her father to take her to the market to have a uniform made. The first day she showed up in the KGSA uniform, the girls smiled at her.

When the results of the exams came back, Lynn was sixteenth out of thirty-two in the first-year class. She passed. It was then that Lynn told herself she would be in the top spot by the next exam period.

"If I can be number sixteen without going to class, surely I can be number one when I do go."

Asha approached Lynn one day at lunch, pointed to her *chapati* and asked, "Can I have some?"

"Yeah," Lynn said, tearing off a quarter.

After lunch that day, Asha offered Lynn her desk. Lynn, without a desk, had been taking notes on her lap.

"Now this is yours. I will look for somewhere else to sit."

"Thanks," Lynn said.

Asha walked around the room asking girls to share their chairs with her. Asha and Lynn have been close friends ever since.

With her new goal to rise from sixteenth to first in her class, Lynn got up at four every morning and read until 5:30. And within one term, she was in the top academic spot. Her next goal was to stay in the top three every term at KGSA. Teka, seeing her tenacity, named her a prefect as well as secretary of the school board. Elated, Lynn didn't tell anyone at KGSA her childhood story. She didn't want their pity; she wanted their respect.

Lynn was born in Mombasa and lived at a corporate dumpsite bordering the ocean for five years. She ventured to the railway line to watch trains, played in the sand, and swam in the ocean. The best treat she found in the rubble was macaroni.

Lynn moved to Kitale when she was five so she could start primary school, but with no money for tuition, she sold vegetables to neighbors instead. She ate the vegetables that were too old to sell and dreamt of sleeping on a bed. While her parents were away at work, Lynn was raped by a neighbor's brother. "I didn't tell anyone. I thought maybe they wouldn't believe me. Maybe I would be beaten up again. Maybe my father would think that I was careless."

She moved again, this time to her grandmother's farm in Lokichogio, where she started third grade and stayed until eighth. She woke at 4:00 a.m. to do chores and start the long walk to school. "If I missed class, I was in very big shit," Lynn laughed.

Lynn's third-grade teacher was very harsh. She would hit the kids on their hands for every wrong answer. Ten wrong meant ten strokes. This didn't bode well for Lynn, who had never been to school before.

"I didn't know how to read and write yet, so she'd beat the hell out of me when I made mistakes. On one math test, I got a 10 percent, and she made me lay on a table. She took a blue and white rod and beat me in front of my classmates, who all laughed at me. Since that day I've never gotten less than 50 percent on a test."

Her home life wasn't much better. Her aunt beat her for sneaking candy. Her grandmother got angry from time to time about having to care for Lynn without compensation—Lynn's father hadn't given Lynn's grandmother her dowry price. She'd yell, "If your father does not give me cows, you are going to be miserable. You will never have a happy life. You just like to stress me, don't you?"

Lynn kept her head down. She did well in school and got a 357 on her KCPE exam. That score could get her into provincial secondary school, but the 20,900 shillings, about $250, for secondary tuition was out of the question. Her grandmother called all Lynn's aunts who were working and asked them for support. Her aunts said they couldn't manage.

Lynn, her sister, and her parents ended up in Kibera in 2007. She was supposed to start school right away. Her father's wages as an artist paid just enough for food and rent. Her mother met a man who offered her tuition money if she'd sleep with him, and she said no. She came home and told Lynn, "I tried my best, but you have to stay home."

Lynn resigned herself to the fact that she was not going to secondary school. She took a job as a live-in babysitter for a five-year-old girl. At the end of the month, the woman of the house took Lynn to the grocery store and told her she could have anything. "Can I have food stamps to give my mother instead?" she asked.

Lynn's second job was in the home of a wealthy Asian woman. Lynn washed utensils, cleaned the house, washed the clothes, and took the kids on walks. She was paid 100 shillings, about one U.S. dollar, at the end of every day. After a few weeks, Lynn was let go because the family was traveling. She stayed at home and waited for the next job. Some days, there was food, other days, there wasn't. The landlady started to threaten eviction. Her father printed T-shirts for 100 shillings a day, and they survived on that for a year.

Lynn was markedly smart. She spoke well in three languages, loved to read, and was curious. Rumors of her high KCPE scores floated around.

"What a shame she is not going to school," neighbors said as they shook their heads, until one neighbor told Lynn about KGSA.

"It's a girls' school, and I think the fees are low."

"Let's try. If they ask for the money, just say we will pay later," Lynn said.

Lynn's father took off work the next day to bring her to KGSA. When they arrived, she saw the mud walls and turned to her father and said, "Is this the school?" Moments later, Claris told her the school was free, and Teka told her she could start at 10:00 a.m.

Mud school or not, Lynn knew she wanted to get a good education. Her grandmother had told her over and over to stay in school, work hard, get a good job, and help support her parents; then, and only then, should she consider getting married and having her own family. Boys weren't going to be a distraction from her learning. Lynn was focused. Men in Kibera tried to lure her—she was gorgeous and carried herself with an attractive confidence—but she ignored them completely.

Claris and Teka would sometimes use money to motivate their students. "The first person to get a calculation is going to get a present." Lynn put her head down and worked to be the first one finished every time.

"If I was given 100 shillings I was happy because I knew that for the next two weeks I could buy kerosene for my lantern. I could buy water for myself, or a candle and soap for washing my uniform. That is how I learned to love mathematics."

CREATING SOMETHING NEW
2009

When you follow in the path of your father, you learn to walk like him.
—ASHANTI PROVERB

By 2009, KGSA was full. Four classes arrived at the beginning of the school year: twenty fourth years, thirty-three third years, and thirty in both years one and two. To accommodate the growing student body, the staff grew to fifteen people, and the monthly salary increased to 7,000 shillings, or eighty-two U.S. dollars. Vision Africa dropped its funding because of their own financial strife, but Sporting Chance gave more. Meanwhile, the MSID students raised over $5,000 for the school, helping to increase the budget to $30,520. By the end of the year, twenty girls took their KCSE exams and graduated in the inaugural class.

Many of the first students at KGSA will tell you that 2009 was the year when things got better. It was a turning point in the collective conscience of the girls. Each year, with more girls and teachers, the school felt more official, more formal. The increasing teachers' salaries helped to retain a few talented teachers. The building grew to accommodate learning. The girls were proud to wear their KGSA uniform around Kibera. With food, tuition, and menstrual pads covered, attention shifted to strengthening classroom performance.

Asha will tell you what she thought was the most important change in the life of the school that year: KGSA chose to take a stand on corporal punishment. Culturally, caning a child was acceptable in both homes and schools in Kenya. Teachers caned their students because they were caned as students. Parents expected it from teachers. They wanted their children to be kept in line. In Kibera, pressures ran high. There were a lot of people living in small homes, packed densely together. There was no privacy and no quiet. People were hungry and a little desperate. People of different tribes and different religions shared space. This led to a culture of casual violence.

"It's draining," Jamie remembered. "It's in your face all the time. Letting people live in poverty is economic violence, and what results from that is physical violence. Homes are violent. Schools are violent. I could throw research at the KGSA teachers, but in actuality, if you hit a kid, the kid sits down."

Teka and Claris were two of the harshest teachers. They were also two of the most respected teachers. In Claris's math class, she set the testing goal at 85 percent. The girls got caned for every point under 80 percent they earned on the exams. The girls worked for that 80 percent.

One day, Lynn looked down at her math paper and smiled: 78 percent. She thought, finally, she was in the clear.

"Lynn, why are you smiling? What have you gotten?" Claris asked.

"Seventy-eight."

"What was the target?"

"Eighty."

"I am going to beat you for not getting those two marks. No pleading. You are going to get those two marks. Stupid mistakes and silly mistakes. Now, give me your hand."

Most of the students took this treatment as motivation. They wanted to get a high mark. They wanted to please their teachers. But there's a stigma in Kibera that girls can't understand math and science, and many KGSA students came in believing they couldn't do math. The beatings intensified this belief.

Asha said, "We walk into class having not eaten breakfast. We are stressed, and our parents have beaten us the night before. And a teacher who then beats us some more doesn't care where we have been and what we are fighting to learn."

When Asha was class representative, she came to school one day to find Teka very unhappy with her class's exam scores. He took them out into the sunny courtyard and told them to kneel. This was another popular punishment. The kneeler became a visual deterrent to other students. Rocks dug into her kneecaps over time. Asha's classmates looked to her, and she said, "We must do what we are told. We are learning for free."

She had recently gone head-to-head with Teka about the girls being punished harshly. He, truly thinking it was the way to motivate their performance, threatened her education. He reminded her that the teachers can chase the girls away from the school for defiance or low performance, and then they were done. There were no other free secondary schools for girls. She knew he was right. If her father paid tuition, then her father, who never beat her at home and was against corporal punishment, could complain and threaten to pull Asha out of school. Because other schools ran on tuition payments, he would be a powerful stakeholder. At KGSA, though, Asha knew it was tougher for her to stand up for her rights.

Asha was a second-year student in 2009 and the head of her class. Even though she was risking getting kicked out of school, she decided to take on the issue. First, she focused on teachers who sent girls away from school because of performance. She reminded the teachers about the ten girls who got sent away as first-year students for failing. "Where did those girls go? They got married! This is not the school Abdul envisioned. You can't tell girls they are too dumb to be helped and send them away. When I see those girls now, they run away because they are ashamed."

Next she addressed the actual beatings.

"Maybe we are failing because of being beaten. I fail at math and get beaten with an electric cable. So I hate math. It doesn't make me want to try harder. I'm afraid. I can't work. It reminds me of home. If you come at me with a cane, I won't listen. You are teaching me how to be rude, and I'm already good at that. But if you talk to me about working hard, I will always remember what you say. I will listen."

She got suspended twice for these speeches, but she didn't back down. She admitted being rude, even calling teachers names, but she wanted to prove to them that she would have no respect for someone who beat her to feel superior, elder or not. She decided to bring the issue straight to Abdul. At first, she had been afraid of Abdul. To her, he seemed larger than life with his big body, boisterous voice, and serious disposition. After watching him for a year, she began to understand him. She believed he saw the students as daughters, that KGSA was his family.

She reasoned with Abdul, "Have the teachers give us punishment, like cleaning the school, but don't let them beat us." She told him her own story from home, of how her mother burned her hand on a kerosene lamp. She told Abdul about how her mother beat her all the time, but never got anything out of her. Even worse, Asha stopped respecting her. Conversely, her father had all her respect for listening to her and reasoning with her.

Her father tried to talk to her mother saying, "These kids have brains. There must be a reason why God gave us brains. A sheep does not have a brain like us. That is why it gets beaten. These children have brains. Don't beat them like that. Sometimes I talk to them and they change because they feel guilty and they understand."

Asha told Abdul that when she was beaten at school, it brought back feelings from being beaten at home. "Beating cannot change people. Beating me because I failed math will not make me get a good grade. It will make me hate it. Do you think punishing me will make me want to do homework? This is inhumane. Even under the UN charter, we have rights as children to be protected."

Abdul saw the logic in Asha's argument. He knew that beatings in primary school, secondary school, and at home were culturally acceptable, but he also knew that what the teachers hoped to get from their students by caning them was not what they got.

He made his position clear to the faculty, but then the beatings would just temporarily stop when he was around the school and continue when he was at Telkom. They were savvy enough to refrain from canings when foreign volunteers were around.

Abdul accepted Asha's idea to have a school board formed. She ran for president and won. Abdul said to her, "These girls have trusted you with their lives. I'm not always here. You need to tell me when the teachers aren't doing their jobs. I know Teka is protecting his teachers. He is pro-corporal punishment."

Abdul asked Asha to tell him when his teachers beat students. She did, which led to tension between her and the faculty. Asha took her leadership role very seriously. If it was her job to lead the students, she was going to stand up for them. The KGSA girls thought Asha was a little crazy for taking on the issue of corporal punishment. But deep down, she knew if she spoke to Abdul he would listen.

Foreign volunteers, not used to seeing violence in school, also told Abdul when corporal punishment occurred. One day, an American volunteer named Carol-Ann ran upstairs from the office to a classroom to get a zip drive from Teka. She heard a commotion, and then a student ran straight into her while trying to escape from the classroom. The girl was crying. And there was Teka, holding an electrical cord.

Carol-Ann was very upset and called Abdul. They acted quickly, calling a mandatory meeting the next morning with all the teachers. She asked about pressing charges on Teka, but she knew this was not the long-term solution.

"It was intense," Carol-Ann remembered. "The girls love the teachers who are beating them. School is free. They are getting beaten. That equation adds up to them. And the teachers are under resourced. They just don't know what else to do."

Abdul felt the divisiveness of the issue and sat all the major stakeholders down for a meeting. The only way it would truly stop is if the teachers could believe in the advantages of not beating the students. He stood in front of the faculty and made a huge, sweeping "U" shape in front of his body with his hand.

"This is the range of options you have to deal with your students, yet you turn to hitting them. Let's brainstorm all the positives that come out of beating students," he said. "If we can come to consensus on the postoperative outcomes of corporal punishment, we will keep it as a policy."

Many of the girls cried at the meeting. They didn't like the disruption at their school, a place they loved. They cried because they were confused. They believed they shouldn't be hit, but they also felt they were strong enough to handle it and didn't want to cause conflict. But by the end of the meeting, the teachers were starting to see how the beatings led to a rift between teachers and students. The school couldn't be a family. The faculty voted to end corporal punishment at KGSA.

The students did not act out when the caning stopped, as some of the teachers feared. Abdul talked to the students, asked them to be responsible, and they were. Slowly, Abdul started to see a change in the relationship between teachers and students. "This is a home for these girls, a safe home. We don't want a home where they get beaten all the time."

Abdul is not the only hero of the KGSA story, but this is one place where Abdul has been indisputably essential. Within a culture where it is perfectly acceptable for a parent to beat a child, or a teacher to beat a student, KGSA has zero tolerance. Abdul changed the minds of parents, teachers, and students to reach this consensus. It led to real and lasting change. It was a defining moment in the story of KGSA.

Teka and Claris have come to see that there is a better way to motivate the girls to learn. Now, all the girls also understand that they deserve better and learn more when they are not scared. Becoming countercultural in Kibera by having no tolerance for violence was galvanizing for the whole KGSA family. They were taking a pivotal stand, and they were doing it together. The teachers asked, "How do I get the attention of a girl who is used to being hit? What kind of consequences can we give that will bring about change? What does positive reinforcement look like?" Within Kibera, KGSA is building a brand-new model of education.

A very charismatic person—a person who can reason with and persuade others—must instigate that kind of cultural shift; a person who himself can inspire enough fear and respect in the other stakeholders that even dissenters are willing to try something new; a person with the perfect mix of compassion and power. Fortunately, Abdul is such a person. He stuck to an unpopular vision until everyone could see its merit.

If it is not okay at KGSA, where is it okay? Abdul's mini-revolution seeped into the community. Maybe now the girls will not hit their own future children. Maybe now, if they become teachers, they will not hit their students.

Teka went from being the biggest believer in corporal punishment to enforcing the new policy as principal. Through it all, no one ever questioned his dedication to the girls. Defending and protecting them was his job. From requiring uniforms to offering free feminine hygiene pads to starting after-school clubs, the girls' safety was always driving his daily decisions.

When a student showed up at Teka's house in bare feet, he gave her his slippers, and she used them as school shoes. When a student told Teka she was pregnant, begging him to let her stay in school, he ensured care for the baby when she returned. When a student came to his house asking for money to buy pads so she didn't have to have sex with boys, Teka gave her his own money. "She only needed fifty shillings," he said, less than sixty cents. "I wanted the girls to wait. I wanted the boys to think twice before approaching a KGSA student, knowing she was strong."

When a student's performance was affected by violence at home, Teka intervened with the parents. When a teacher's drinking problem put students at risk, Teka fired the teacher. Angry and intoxicated, the fired teacher took the students' notebooks as he stormed away. Teka pursued him and ended up in the hospital after the man hit him on the nose.

"This scar is my KGSA wound," Teka said. "I had to fight for the girls to get their notebooks back."

Kiberans hear gunshots weekly. Girls get harassed daily. One day, Teka caught a grown man peeking into the latrine to watch the girls use the toilet. Another day, he caught a young boy who had scaled the fence and broken a window to steal things from a classroom. He couldn't call the police and couldn't afford a lawyer. The police and politicians have turned their backs on Kibera. Teka felt a daily responsibility to protect his students. He maintained a contradictory persona—one that allowed the girls to feel safe around him but scared potential thieves and peepers away.

Managing the clubs was one creative way that Teka kept the girls safe. They stayed at school a few extra hours each day, learning new skills. The clubs were fairly informal, but the year 2009 saw some important changes. A new third-year transfer student, Ida, brought her intensity to the position of president of the Journalism Club.

The Journalism Club met every Saturday and was very informal. They collected news and read it during the morning assembly at school to the other students.

Asha's first memory of Journalism Club was Ida barging into her classroom and yelling at the second-year members, "You are working in my club and you are not producing. I'm going to fire you. Emergency meeting at four!"

Ida was a wiry soccer player with an easy fashion sense and a quick, witty sass. She was a slight young woman with light brown skin and a short, stiff ponytail. She wore a soccer jersey under a cardigan and fidgeted with a set of keys when she spoke, while staring off into the distance. Ida spoke eloquently and fiercely in three languages. An intense student/athlete with a willpower second to none at the school, Ida was a born leader.

Ida had four brothers and three sisters and joked that, with eight kids, her parents were trying to make their very own soccer team. When she was in eighth grade, her father told her that she would stay home after graduating primary school. He planned to send only her brothers on for more schooling.

She found KGSA, which she knew was a catalyst for her dreams. Behind her intensity was a drive to prove her father wrong by graduating from secondary school and building a career. KGSA offered Ida an education and she excelled. She wanted more. She wanted to go to college. Her first act as president of the Journalism Club was to make the club English-speaking-only. Knowing that English was a marketable skill the girls needed to improve upon, she kicked girls out for speaking in Swahili. They started by meeting after school to write news articles they would then read at the morning meetings in the courtyard.

Ida was hard on Asha, and Asha loved it. Ida and Asha became fast friends and colleagues. When Ida claimed she would become president of Kenya, Asha believed her. Ida mentored Asha and became a role model. Asha would follow in Ida's footsteps, stepping into similar leadership roles with her own moxie.

Under Ida's leadership and vision, the Journalism Club started writing articles for their own school newspaper. Seeing the same intensity in Asha that she saw in herself, Ida quickly named her editor of the school paper. Then they got the opportunity to work with an organization that would put them on the international map. Carol-Ann Gleason, who had advocated for the elimination of corporal punishment after seeing it in action, was at KGSA as the program manager of Geo-Girls: Citizen Journalism from New York. She wanted KGSA's Journalism Club to partner with Geo-Girls.

Geo-Girls connected indigenous girls in Chiapas, Mexico, girls from the Lower East Side Girls' Club in New York City, and KGSA girls in Kibera through writing. Carol-Ann brought Danielle St. Laurent, a fashion photographer, along with her to train the girls. They gave the school a laptop equipped with media programs. In three weeks of after-school workshops, they taught the girls basic journalism techniques with point-and-shoot cameras. They also brought the girls to an Internet cafe so they could see their photography on big screens. Some girls were drawn to Danielle and wanted to learn everything they could about photography. Others, including Asha, were drawn to the writing aspect of the project. Carol-Ann loved Geo-Girls because the girls were the technicians and producers. They got to tell their own stories however they wanted. She hoped that power would disrupt and challenge the preexisting narratives about girls in poverty and highlight the dynamic voices and vibrant stories of the KGSA students.

Jake Naughton, a junior at the University of Wisconsin at Madison, in Kenya with MSID, was a gifted photographer and media specialist. Jake helped Teka, Carol-Ann, and Danielle facilitate meetings after school. They taught the girls how to take stills and video shots and how to edit. One of their first projects was on water in honor of World Water Day.

"Club meetings were pretty riotous at times, and at other times completely dead," Jake said. "I think it was very unclear what benefit the girls saw out of Journalism Club in any practical way. Many of them wanted to become news anchors on television because it was a way to gain fame and get out of Kibera. We spent most of those first few meetings trying to brainstorm potential topics and story ideas for the Geo-Girls projects, training them in basic composition and camera techniques and thinking about how to tell a story about a place you are so familiar with but that is so misunderstood by anyone outside of Kibera."

After Carol-Ann and Danielle left, Jake and Teka continued to train the girls to strengthen their presence with Geo-Girls. The media training transitioned to teaching the girls how to create their own stories and upload them to the Web. It pushed the girls to want more.

Jake said, "I think eventually the girls saw the power behind journalism. They embraced their roles as muckrakers, understanding themselves as agents of change."

Teka worked with the other clubs to up the intensity as well. He trained the supervising teachers to treat them more like training camps than clubs. Drama Club started taking the girls to competitions outside of Kibera to perform. They sent the girls in Poetry Club to five weeks of training with Nadia Kist, a poet from New York who was in Nairobi as a founder of Seeds for Hope. At the end of the training, they performed their poetry for a paying audience. The Science Club started competing too. They learned how to make shoe polish out of kerosene and how to gather plastic bags, clean them, and weave them into handbags to sell.

"We told the girls they could make it. We didn't want to watch them go back to the same houses they came from, four years older, but no more ready to earn wages. The girls in Kibera used to think they were good only for dating and getting married," Teka said. "They never believed in themselves, and no one ever believed in them. But things are changing."

While Teka kept the girls safe during the school day, Abdul wanted to move the school funding to the next level. Living "hand to mouth," as he called it, was exhausting and scary. So many of the girls were in crisis. Abdul was paying out of his own pocket for emergencies and sometimes teachers' salaries, when he himself had so little. What he dreamed of was a discretionary fund. He needed a source of money that was not in the form of a grant. When organizations like PADEM or Sporting Chance gave money, it was always restricted funds given for a specific purpose. The money needed to be used accordingly and reported accurately. Abdul wanted access to money he could use for emergency purposes without having to ask for permission. It needed to come from people who trusted him to spend it wisely as needed for the benefit of the girls. When the MSID graduates wanted to do more, Abdul realized that they could build this discretionary fund for him.

Money had been trickling in from the United States since 2006 when Shaun, the first MSID volunteer at KGSA, and his friend Ryan returned home. They each had their own methods of raising money. Shaun bought twenty-four cartons of soda and sold the cans individually for profit. Ryan threw parties at his house and sold jewelry and Kenyan cloth to his friends. Jamie's family became invested in the school and Aisling did a photography show with her own pictures of Kibera in a coffee shop in Madison. They wired Abdul the money, but they were always thinking about how to do more.

Abdul, Shaun, Jamie, and Ryan had several conversations about the MSID alums forming a nonprofit in the United States to support the school until it could support itself. Abdul trusted them because they had all spent significant time at the school with the girls. They had been honest with him, following through with money when they said they could and telling him no when they couldn't. They trusted Abdul to make smart decisions on the ground with the money. And with the MSID-KGSA partnership, there would be a growing number of MSID alums to expand the support team in the United States.

Carol-Ann helped Ryan navigate the legal side of setting up a foundation and recommended that Jake get involved as well. Ryan's father gave him books on entrepreneurship and nonprofits, and Ryan begged his roommate to stay up late into the night talking about how to build the KGSA Foundation. His mentors kept reminding him to build a structure that didn't foster dependence—development shouldn't be seen as a career, but rather as a way to transfer skills. It was about training and serving as a resource.

From the beginning, they wanted the KGSA Foundation to play a secondary role to the school. "The mission of the Foundation has always been the same—to reduce or eliminate gender inequality and poverty through partnership with KGSA. We as an organization could give KGSA more credibility and accountability through the board while allowing Abdul and the Kibera community to proceed as they saw fit. We would not micromanage him, but support him."

First, with pictures from Danielle, they launched a website where people could donate to the school. They called it KGSA Inc., but because it wasn't registered with the IRS as an official charity, the money was not tax deductible and went straight into an account Ryan set up. He then wired the money to Abdul.

Next, KGSA Inc. partnered with an umbrella organization called Omprakash. They support smaller movements by granting them access to their 501(c)3 status. It was nice to have donations be tax deductible, but it was confusing to donors to write a check out to Omprakash with KGSA in the memo line. It wasn't a long-term solution, but they were able to contribute $5,570 to KGSA in 2009, one-sixth of the school's total budget for that year.

While his friends went out to bars on Friday nights, Ryan sat at his father's dining room table, surrounded by books, mission statements, and vision statements, and dug in. He asked his roommate Danny to stay home and drink whiskey with him and talk about nonprofits.

"How would you do this?"

Danny talked for a bit, trying to be supportive, before he said, "Stay home a while longer. But then get your ass out by 11:30 and let's play darts."

Meanwhile, Ryan and his girlfriend planned a trip to Kenya in the fall of 2009. He decided to work on an official partnership between KGSA and the supporters in the United States. They stayed for ten months. With this return trip, it became clear that Ryan was leading the charge by the American foundation. The others helped him set priorities for his time in Kenya, including finding books for the school.

Stepping off the plane in Nairobi, Ryan was full of emotions. Memories of his study-abroad time came back with the heat, smells, and accents of the Kenyans. He was worried that Abdul wouldn't recognize him. He exited the customs area and searched the line of Kenyans, five people deep, waiting to pick up arriving loved ones. He didn't see Abdul. Then, seemingly out of nowhere, a huge man ran right up to him.

"Brother!" Abdul yelled. "Welcome home." He embraced Ryan before he had time to respond.

After getting settled, Ryan called Teka.

"You are here?" Teka asked.

"Yeah, I'm here. I'd love to come see the school."

"Okay, I'll send two students to come get you. Meet them where you and I used to meet."

Ryan saw two girls in navy uniforms come walking around the bend, giggling. The two students greeted Ryan and led him to KGSA. Walking through Kibera for the first time in three years, Ryan didn't know quite what to expect. The last time he had been at the school, it had been in the first location. He had only seen pictures of the new building.

When he went through the last gate that opens up into the courtyard of the school, he started crying. "It was an amazing sight to see what they had done as a school. These were all connections that Abdul himself made. He found the filmmaker who brought PADEM in. Nothing about any of that were partnerships through MSID."

Abdul took Ryan into the lab. PADEM came in for year two of their three-year financial commitment with $22,000, which the school used to build a laboratory. Of the twenty high schools in the area, only eight had laboratories and six of those were in private religious schools. It helped set KGSA apart. They had come a long way from dirt floors and plastic chairs. Abdul took him upstairs to the library PADEM had funded. At that moment, the four old computers were all working.

"Wow. We have Internet in Kibera. The girls have access to a lot of information."

PADEM built the library, but their funding did not cover filling it with books. They built the lab, but they didn't cover the cost of chemicals. Ryan looked to MSID for help. Three MSID alums had started an organization called Books Build Hope. If Books Build Hope could raise $15,000 for shipping, Books for Africa would give schools of their choice 25,000 books. Ryan got KGSA on this list. Books Build Hope raised the first $7,000 with small fundraisers in the United States. They needed $8,000 more.

Around that time, a team from the University of Minnesota travelled to KGSA on a tour of MSID sites. They were immediately impressed by the enrollment and the safe space the school had created. Robert Jones, a senior vice president, was struck by Abdul's tenacity, Teka's ability to do a lot with limited resources, and the innovative and ingenious model of using soccer to rally around education. When Abdul explained that their food funding had recently been cut, everyone looked at each other, took out their wallets, and donated every shilling they had on the spot.

Abdul and Ryan gave them a tour. After seeing the classrooms and office, Abdul asked Robert, "Would you like to see our library?"

They walked upstairs and entered a long, rectangular room with butcher-block tables, four old desktop computers and a wall of empty shelves.

Robert asked, "Where are all the books?"

"We don't know yet. We need to find some money to take advantage of a Books for Africa shipment."

"Oh, the CEO of Books for Africa is a good friend of mine," Robert said. "I'll take care of it when I go home."

Two different departments at the University of Minnesota came together to donate the money to cover not just KGSA's share, but the rest of the shipment cost for all the schools in the Books Build Hope network. Twenty-five thousand books were distributed to eleven different secondary schools. Finally, the shelves in the library at KGSA were full.

Sending a daughter to secondary school is very expensive for a family in Kibera. When families are making mere dollars a day, every potential wage earner counts, and a daughter in school is one less wage coming in, as well as one more mouth to feed. Teka and Abdul told parents that for every year a girl stays in school, her wage-earning potential goes up 10–20 percent, which is true.

"We will give her lunch, we will give her pads, and she will eventually be able to help the entire family," Teka said.

This is also true. Even so, Teka and Abdul knew that it was a race against time; parents who desperately need money may not be able to afford to hold out for more money later. With no safety net, the margin for error was very small for these families. At the same time, the rewards could be great: Every year a girl stayed in school, every year a girl put off pregnancy, was one more step away from prostitution, illness, and poverty and toward solvency, independence, and health.

Absent fathers made the financial pressures on daughters more intense. Some fathers were working upcountry, some were dead, and others were just gone. When Rose's father died, her mother went to her relatives in Nairobi for financial help so Rose could stay in school. They made promises, but never came through. Rose had to find work off and on washing clothes, but when there was no work, there was no food. She'd eat the lunch at KGSA, but go without breakfast and dinner.

"We didn't have time to study, because we were looking for work," she explained. "And then at school, we couldn't think about the subject matter because we were worried about where we were going to find work."

She felt constant pressure to drop out and get married. Boys were supposed to get educated to help out the family. Girls were supposed to get married to help out the family.

"But I believe all children are equal. Educate the girl child, and maybe she will help the family. You never know who will help," Rose said in a matter-of-fact way.

She began to believe that soccer, not school, was her ticket out of the slum. Rose was gaining a reputation in Kibera for her soccer skills. "They called me a celeb and said I'd be famous someday. Boys loved to come watch me play."

She eventually chose one of the boys to be her boyfriend, and she got pregnant the first time they had sex. When she told him, he asked her to marry him. She said no. Three months later, he upped the stakes.

"Marry me or I'm leaving."

"I'm too young to get married. My mother will take care of me. I'll be fine."

Rose was worried that if she married him, she would keep having children that she could not support. She decided to be a single mother with the support of her own mother. She took two months off after giving birth to her daughter and then returned to school and soccer at KGSA.

Around the same time, Faridah got pregnant too. Worried about how her community would react, she closed herself off in her home when her belly started to grow.

After a few days, she heard a knock on the door. It was Teka and her soccer mates.

Teka invited her to come back to school. KGSA supported her through the pregnancy, and she went into labor late in 2009. When the pain started getting worse, she went to the hospital.

"Your time has come," they said.

"Oh, my God. How am I going to do it?"

The woman sharing a room with Faridah was crying out so loudly in pain it scared her. She started praying.

"At first, I couldn't believe it was my son. I was happy to hold him, and I realized, 'I am a parent.'" She named her son Ashley Coal after a soccer player for Chelsea, a famous professional team out of London.

One month after giving birth, she separated from her boyfriend. He didn't come around very often, but when he did he treated her like he owned her because of their child. He started seeing other women, confident that she would depend on him.

She told him, "I'll do my best to raise my son. Don't bother. I can do it without you."

Faridah's and Rose's decisions to be single moms broke a lot of cultural norms. Faridah's parents had an arranged marriage. She felt pressure to marry the father of her son, but she didn't want him to control her life. She liked her job at KGSA and saw the benefits of working. She believed that working gave her self-respect. She wanted to keep making her own money and her own decisions. Teka hired her back to work for the microfinance program. She is raising her son on her own as a proud working mother.

"Before I gave birth, I felt like a girl. Now, I have to wash my clothes, wash my son's clothes, and feed him. I'm not a girl. I'm a mother. With time I would like a daughter, but not now. When I am ready, I will ask God for a girl. I would love to have two kids and that is it. With our life in Kibera, you can't have too many kids."

The KCSE is a test all secondary students in Kenya take. It takes the entire month of November for the students to complete. Eight subjects are covered across twenty-seven tests. The girls wait until February, sometimes as late as April to receive a composite score out of 100. That number will determine whether they can go on to get a certificate, diploma, or degree in post-secondary education. With a D–, D, or D+, students are eligible for certificate courses that tend to lead to low-paying jobs like catering or secretarial work. A C– or C allows the students to apply to two-year diploma courses. A C+ or above qualifies them to apply to four-year degree courses, but the test score doesn't guarantee a spot. There are currently seventy thousand openings in Kenya's public universities each year, so if one hundred thousand students score a C+ or above, they have to compete for the available spots. The students apply to a certain department at a particular school and then wait to hear if they are accepted. A student may be accepted into the school but placed in a different department studying an unexpected academic discipline.

This is all assuming, of course, that the student can pay the tuition. The KGSA students cannot pay for secondary, let alone post-secondary, education. So if you ask a KGSA student about her goal on the KCSE, she will say a B, because a B or above qualifies her for government loans and scholarships.

The lab at KGSA was built too late in 2009 to benefit the first group of students taking their KCSE. The building didn't meet the regulations required to host the test, so the 2009 graduates carried their desks across Kibera to St. Gabriel's, a recognized high school. It was a twenty-five minute walk. "The classrooms had open windows so mosquitoes came in and bit us," Linet remembered. "There was sewage in front of the classroom, so it smelled. Not great testing conditions."

Once the twenty girls got settled, Teka and Abdul gathered them together before the test to help them get centered. A few of the girls, Linet and Rose included, had been with Abdul from the very beginning, four years before.

Abdul just said, "Look, I know this was not an ideal four years. It was not what you thought secondary school should be. But I don't want you to forget the great accomplishments you have been able to achieve. Look at where you are at right now. Look at what you have been through. We are all incredibly proud of you. Regardless of what happens, you still have a family and a community at KGSA. Just because you are done with exams doesn't mean you need to leave this family. We will figure this out together. It doesn't stop here."

Twenty girls took the KCSE and graduated from KGSA. Then they waited for the results.

Abdul said, "The strength of this whole institution is the girls themselves. Their commitment makes me want to do more. It's always sad when a group graduates. KGSA is more than a school. It's a home. It's healthy. I know they carry so much with them when they leave, not only education, but also life, respect, and a way of living. They need that.

"I fear when the girls do not get into university. Being eighteen and being done with school isn't ideal, but it's better than at fourteen. They are focused. We help replace empty minds with open minds, minds that can make sound judgments and sound decisions."

Queen was never top in her class. She struggled quite a bit after the postelection violence and missed a lot of school. As a third-year student, she got pregnant, gave birth to a baby girl, and came back to KGSA to finish. She just barely passed her KCSE.

None of the 2009 class scored high enough to go on to postsecondary school. Their education was coming to an end. Or so Abdul thought.

Linet came to see Abdul and said, "I want to sit for fourth year a second time. I want to take the KCSE again. I know I can improve and go to college."

They agreed. Josephat was heading to college in 2010, but Abdul encouraged him to teach at KGSA on his breaks and holidays. Josephat continued to support Linet on his KGSA teacher's salary so she could repeat her final year.

At the end of each of the three terms each year, KGSA had a closing ceremony. The girls cleaned out their desks while the teachers double-checked their grading. Teka played reggae music on his laptop and rented speakers, and the girls danced in the courtyard. An opening prayer was followed by dances and poems performed by students. Teachers talked to them about how to conduct themselves over the break: "Avoid boys" and "read your books."

Finally, what the girls had all been waiting for arrived: The teacher representing the first years read off the top three performers and handed out prizes. The other three classes followed suit. A closing prayer ended the ceremony before a special lunch of meat, rice, and cheese. It was a special day of celebration and closure, filled with light-hearted laughter and a brief moment of abundance.

In December, at the end of the third term, KGSA's first graduation ceremony occurred. The KGSA Foundation provided funds to make it a grand affair. Lynn's father was commissioned to create a huge banner to hang from the second-floor balcony saying, "Congratulations Graduates." A big tent shaded the dirt courtyard. A feast of food including chicken and dessert awaited. Families shuffled in, proud to be attending a high school graduation for their daughters.

Abdul, Teka, and Ryan all spoke with red-rose boutonnieres pinned to their finest shirts. Prizes and graduation plaques were awarded to each graduate. Queen, Jacqueline, and Nancy, some of the very first students at KGSA, made it. Some were graduating only with a D–. Queen had her daughter in her lap during the ceremony. They were proud. They were graduating.

ACCESSING THE LIGHT

2010

Luxury is one thing, but with a pen, I can reach people's minds.

—ASHA JAFFAR

The year 2010 was the kind of year that required Abdul's long-term vision as well as his patience. It appeared on the surface that not much was happening at KGSA. But the explosion of growth in 2011 would never have happened without the slow, patient work of 2010.

PADEM came in for the third and final year of their contract with $22,000. The money went toward the teachers' salaries, materials for the laboratory, and helped the first graduating class pay and register for national exams. Sporting Chance remained the longest-standing donor to KGSA. The KGSA Foundation doubled their efforts and contributed over $11,000 to the budget. Abdul and Teka brought new partner organizations onboard as well, growing the budget of the school to $37,000.

With PADEM on the way out, Abdul met a Dutch couple at a strategic time. Back in 2001, John Schut and Linda Janssen started a foundation called Stichting 4 Life (Foundation 4 Life in English). They hired HIV-positive single mothers in Kibera to make jewelry, which was sold in Holland at big department stores. Stichting 4 Life paid a fair wage and also paid for two children in each family to attend school.

When John and Linda wanted to expand the reach of Stichting 4 Life, they looked for soccer programs they could partner with. John was immediately drawn to Abdul's story. They contacted KGSA and visited. They were impressed and saw how KGSA forwarded the values of their foundation. "Abdul takes care of those girls. He could move out of Kibera, but he stays," Linda said. "He has a very big heart, and it is always showing."

They decided to fund KGSA's feeding program in Vision Africa's absence. As their foundation grew, so did their partnership. Stichting 4 Life gave $10,000 to the school.

After graduating from Boston University, Jamie was working for Teach a Man to Fish in Uganda. Teach a Man to Fish was a British organization that helped schools become financially sustainable by starting school businesses. The businesses taught entrepreneurial skills to students while bridging the school-to-work gap. Jamie invited Abdul and Teka to the 2010 conference in Tanzania, knowing that they had been talking about income-generating businesses for years.

It was Teka's first time out of the country. Abdul forgot his passport, but by the time they reached the border, he had made friends with a woman on the bus who had enough connections to get him a temporary passport.

"It was lovely to be around so many people from all over the world who cared about education," Abdul said. "But most of the stories of success included agriculture. There is a school in Paraguay that has three hundred acres of land!"

Abdul stood up during a session and said, "These are all great ideas, but my school is in a slum. What do I do to raise money?" A special session was created because of Abdul's enthusiasm and urgency. Everyone wanted to hear about KGSA. He told the story of the school, and a discussion about self-sustaining urban schools began. He came back from the conference convinced that the after-school clubs could have great potential to generate income. He told the mentors of all the clubs that income generation needed to be one part of their missions. The Journalism Club was ready to take that step.

The Journalism Club motivated students who had become good researchers, writers, editors, and photographers, but Geo-Girls was not generating income. The girls decided to shift their work to produce a magazine. Instead of writing news for their own school, why not write for an audience outside of Kibera? They partnered with Junior Achievement (JA), an international organization that helped young people learn about business and money management, to help move the club toward income generation.

Tim Colburn, a British consultant working with Kenya Airways, was a certified mentor with JA in the U.K. He was looking for volunteer work in Kibera, and the president of JA in Nairobi recommended that Tim mentor KGSA as a JA site.

"We've created the club because we know that many journalists from around the world come to Kibera. They report their stories in their papers. We want to write our story," the girls told Tim on his first day. "We want to contribute, but we aren't quite sure how. We are here because we have ambition."

"Oh," Tim said. "What's your ambition?"

"My name is Beatrice, and I want to be a member of congress."

"My name is Irene, and I am a photographer. I want to be a photojournalist. I take good pictures."

Tim was impressed with the specificity and vividness of the KGSA girls' answers. He worked for Kenya Airways during the week and KGSA on Saturdays to help the Journalism Club structure a company program around JA's guidelines. They had to create a business, identify shareholders, and produce a product to sell.

The second week, Tim asked the girls, "If you could write stories about anything, what would you write? What should other people know?"

They identified themes: Kibera, education for girls, politics, health, business, entertainment, and sports. And those themes became the section of their first magazine.

The third week, they held elections for the section leaders and leadership positions. After impassioned speeches, Ida was voted in as president, Asha as editor, Irene as chief photographer, Joyline as marketing manager, and Lynn as the human resource manager. They each brought ten shillings to the fourth meeting to buy shares in the business. They each received a paper voucher for their share, and they had a bit of capital to work with. The fifth week, the sections met and started giving assignments for the first edition.

Several obstacles became evident immediately. Magazines are expensive and time-consuming to produce. The girls were timid and lacked leadership. Tim worked on convincing them that if they took their journalism skills seriously, they could become an income-generation system. It could help them get a job. They started to see that they were shareholders.

Tim handed over his camera. Each week, Irene and her team took stunning, clever photos. The girls started to show up in their best clothes, some with flowers in their hair, looking good, knowing that cameras would be there. They began posing and coming out of themselves a bit. Each week, Tim took the pictures and made them into a slideshow and set them to music. Then, at the beginning of each meeting, they began by watching the slideshow. Teka brought speakers in to amplify the Kenyan techno music. The girls were enraptured: my face, my photo. They did not look poor and disheveled. They looked sassy, proud, and electric. It brought a sense of possibility and belonging. They made him play it through twice, once to see the pictures and once to dance to the music.

"We can create optimism through journalism, and we are going to blooming well create it. They saw the hope in the pictures they took," Tim said.

On the cover of the first edition was Irene's photo of Rehema, the most junior member of the Journalism Club. She was a twelve-year-old in primary school, but she showed up at meetings nonetheless. In the photo, she wears a gray shirt with the hood up, staring down at the lens with a slight smile. Rehema became known as the cover girl. The product became real and achievable. The motivation was high. They dreamed of it making money and where that money could go.

"What if we put it toward scholarships?"

"What if we give proceeds back to KGSA?"

One Saturday, Tim took a few students into Nairobi with a customer survey to do market research assessing the viability of a magazine as a product. The girls asked people at the Westgate Mall if they would be interested in a magazine about Kibera and how much they would be willing to pay. The girls decided to focus sales in Kibera and in the NGO and international traveler community of Nairobi.

Asha requested meetings with Ryan to work on her editing. Ida made meetings more formal with agendas and deadlines. Tim got a printing company in Nairobi to print 600 copies at cost. They produced their first international magazine.

"We called the magazine *Shedders* because we want to shed light on the situation in Kibera for all the world to see," Asha said.

When the first edition of *Shedders* was ready in February of 2010, Tim brought copies to KGSA with a bag full of celebratory sodas, noisemakers, and snacks for the girls. They fidgeted excitedly in the library while Tim passed a magazine to each of the girls. Some giggled and squealed; others sat in awed silence and turned the pages. It was a dream come true to see their names in print.

Abdul entered the library, and Ida approached him, asking, "Would you like to buy a copy of our magazine?"

"Of course."

"That will be 200 shillings."

Abdul laughed, reaching into his pocket, proud to be the first official sale for the Journalism Club.

The second sale went to a man named Wycliffe. He grew up as

an orphan in Nairobi, sniffing glue and carrying shopping bags to people's cars for loose change to survive. One day he carried the bags of an American who got curious about Wycliffe and ended up paying not only for his secondary education, but also a microloan to start a business. As a successful entrepreneur with a tough background, he enjoyed coming to KGSA to inspire the girls and push them forward in their business venture.

Tim brought guests with him from Kenyan Airways, and so the girls sold their next ten copies of *Shedders* that day to them.

"That was one of the best days for the Journalism Club," Asha remembered fondly.

The club members went out into Kibera and Westgate Mall to sell magazines, but it was harder than they had expected. The magazines didn't sell well. People in Kibera wanted them for free. People in Nairobi and even Tim and Ryan's networks in the U.K. and U.S. respectively offered to make a donation, but they were not as interested in the actual magazine. The first edition broke even. The lack of profit was a disappointment. However, *Shedders* proved to have unintended positive outcomes. Abdul used the magazine, full of impressive visuals and stories, as a marketing and fundraising tool. Tim and Ryan used it to raise awareness and donations in the international community. The legitimate, professional product raised the confidence of the girls and raised the profile of the school. *Shedders* put KGSA on the map.

With *Shedders* as a product, Teka and Ida started preparing the team to compete in their first JA competition. Asha and Ida remembered the first JA competition in Nairobi as being a little awkward. Each business sets up a booth to present their idea outside in a large field. All the other businesses brought materials to decorate the booth. KGSA brought nothing. They sat at an empty white table in folding chairs. Asha and Ida walked around to all the other booths and sized up the competition. Maybe they didn't bring stand decorations, but they came back to report to the other girls that their product and business plan were the best.

While judges assessed the outdoor stands, inside, the executive committee of each business presented the business model to a panel. The top-ten businesses were announced midday, and those ten groups then presented to a new panel of judges in a large auditorium. From there, the top-three high school businesses went on to the national JA competition.

KGSA made the top ten, and when they completed presenting *Shedders* the second time, the auditorium gave them a standing ovation. Asha said, "Everyone was impressed by our confident presentation and our products. Ida was really articulate."

They placed fifth.

Abdul went to the competition in 2010 and was impressed with how KGSA matched up. They were the only school from Kibera competing against big private schools around Nairobi. Some school's business plans were small and cautious. For example, one school sold *mandazi*, fried bread, to make money. KGSA's plan of running an international magazine immediately got the attention of other schools.

"Our girls were still a little bit shy," Abdul critiqued, "but our product was the best. There is a lot of information about Kibera that needs to get out, and they can use the magazine as a vehicle. The business aspect of the club helps them with business and money management. It will help after graduation."

KGSA's fifth-place finish at their first Nairobi competition got people's attention. John Wali, the president of JA in Kenya, came to KGSA to visit the club. KGSA was the first school from a slum to join JA Kenya, and he wanted to keep tabs on what they were up to.

Ida had the club in order, ready to impress him. When he arrived, Ida and Asha presented the first issue of *Shedders* magazine to him. They explained how they came up with the articles. At the end of his visit, John told the girls that Sean Rush, president of JA Worldwide, was coming to Kenya and wanted to meet them.

A week later, Sean Rush announced that he was coming to visit the school.

"We are in deep shit," Teka told the Journalism Club when he got the news. "The JA president is coming to our school from the United

States and the fourth years are not going to be here." The entire class had recently been suspended from school for bad behavior. But Asha wasn't worried. She wasn't easily intimidated.

"I've been to some very difficult places in the world," Sean said, weaving his way through the slum. "But it's always a shock to arrive at a place like Kibera."

Abdul showed Sean around the school while the girls ate lunch in the courtyard.

"KGSA struck me as an oasis. It captivated me right away," he said. "I sensed comfort and safety as well as opportunity."

After lunch, Sean Rush met the Journalism Club in the library. He immediately noticed the empty library shelves. While waiting for the Books Build Hope shipment, the students relied on a few old American textbooks.

Asha spoke up first. "Why did you come to Kibera? You have 180 countries to go see. Why here of all schools?"

"I read *Shedders*. I was inspired by your story. You are from Kibera, but are still determined to go to competitions against the big schools. I didn't have a lavish childhood. I had to struggle and fend for myself. I started working at age twelve. I had a paper route, worked at a gas station, and drove a forklift to pay my way through college. I fought cancer while earning my third master's degree at Harvard. Nothing was handed to me. I have been very impressed with your showing at the Junior Achievement competitions. I respect people who clearly understand work."

Eventually, he asked the group what they needed to succeed. Asha raised her hand and said she wanted books.

"What kind of books do you want?"

"I want to read Obama's books, and I want novels so we can improve our English. We need a laptop to type our articles. We need a printer to print our news."

"What's your name?"

"My name is Asha."

Sean latched onto Asha from this first encounter. "She had

chutzpah—a poise and grace to her that impressed me. She stood out. The others were shy, but she asked me questions." He continued to ask her questions back.

"What do you want to do when you grow up?"

"I want to be a lawyer and a journalist."

"Why?"

"I want to be the voice of the voiceless. In Kenya, for you to be able to look for a lawyer, you have to have a lot of money. I want to study so I can help those people who don't have money. The reason people are stepping on us is because we cannot speak. To speak, you have to have degrees. I will do law as a service. I will do journalism for the money to help me help the people in my area with law."

One of Asha's classmates had once told her that her mother had been raped. She said it as if it was not that serious, like they should expect that kind of life. That moment triggered in Asha a desire to be a lawyer. She wanted to represent people in Kibera who had come to believe they were not worthy of having rights.

She told Sean, "When I say I want to be a lawyer, people will say it is very expensive—6,000 shillings per semester. It's very hard to support a family and pay for school. It's not a realistic dream, but I will be a lawyer. I will do it."

He asked the group about how it felt that the U.S. President was of Kenyan ancestry. He asked about their *Shedders* articles and their lives. Before leaving, Sean asked Abdul, "What do you need?"

"What you see is what we have," Abdul said, "and it's not enough. We need new computers and more books."

"Give me a list of every book you need."

He told John Wali, "All they have is ancient Macs with floppy disks. Half of them don't work. I'm getting these girls some computers before I leave Kenya."

To the surprise of Abdul, Teka, and the Journalism Club girls, Sean Rush was good on his word. He went to a state bookstore in Nairobi and handed the list of titles to an employee.

"I need all of these, and 150 books on the history of Kenya."

He returned to KGSA the next day as promised and delivered the cases of books. He promised Teka and Abdul that computers and cameras were ordered and on their way. He gently placed *The Audacity of Hope* on the table. Asha ran and grabbed the book.

"There you are!" he said to Asha.

"You remembered my wish! Obama! I wanted *Dreams of my Father* too."

He pulled it out of his bag and handed it to her.

The library fell completely silent as the girls paged through their new books. While holding her new books, Asha told Sean about her dream to write. "People may forget what I speak, but the written story will always be there on the shelf. If I go and speak to you, you will hear me in the moment, but you meet a lot of people, and my words will disappear among theirs. The first book I write will be about my mother coming from the refugee camp. People will remember me."

He continued to support her big dreams. When Sean came back to KGSA the third time, he asked her, "Did you like those stories?"

"Yes. We need more books to read."

Every time he is in Kenya, Sean does his best to make time to come to see the girls. Each time, he asks Abdul what he needs.

"Five hundred dollars? You got it. How much is a computer? You got it."

Asha's audacity and charisma continued to inspire Sean to make generous personal donations to KGSA. He said to her, "If you finish secondary school, find me on Facebook and we will talk about your education." She stayed in touch with him by email and began to think of him as a father figure.

Not all outsiders visiting Kibera, though, are looking for potential in the slum. Asha pointed out a group of four older white people. The man translating for them held a huge gun. They looked uncomfortable as they passed out knitted hats to kids on the street. "Why are they afraid of us?" She saw Kibera in a tour guidebook listed as a tourist attraction. "Are dump sites a destination? Are people dying of AIDS and going hungry things to gawk at? Kibera is not a tourist attraction.

Every day when I walk to school I see *mzungus*, white people, around here taking photos. They go to the railway to get the aerial view. They take those photos and exploit us. They make money off the photos. They want to tell the story of how poor we are, how sick we are, how dirty we are."

One day, a famous news anchor, Lilian Muli, came to KGSA to do a segment for her show on Citizen Television. Asha ran up to her long-time journalism idol to introduce herself. She told the anchor she wanted to be just like her someday. Lilian gave Asha a side glance and wouldn't shake her hand. "She just looked me up and down and turned away. They come with their cameras, but they don't care about us. We are only good ratings for them. We are so poor that we are news."

Lilian's Citizen crew had students staged in the library, studiously looking over books or at the computer. A second-year student had a spotlight on her while waiting to be interviewed. Classes had to stop to accommodate the crew.

The segment on KGSA aired on a Saturday night. The segment was part of a repeated series called "Strength of a Woman." KGSA started getting calls immediately from Kenyans wanting to volunteer and donate. But Asha didn't like the piece. "I should be the one telling the story. I could do it better. I know Kibera."

Shedders magazine wants to tell the story of Kibera differently.

The girls have all heard lines written and aired by journalists like these: "Poverty levels are sky high." "It is a seething mass of desperately poor people." "Here, more than one million people live in squalor."

But these sound bites don't convey what they wanted to show: that they are strong and successful. They are smart and talented, but they just need opportunities. They didn't need people to cry over their stories, just to believe in them. "What if we tried to use the positive things? Some people might say, 'These people are living through hell, but they are still smiling and still dancing. They are still working hard. I think we should help them.' That is what made Sean Rush interested. We didn't go crying. We were there and we were poised and told him we wanted to be journalists and lawyers."

With this desire to tell a different story of Kibera, the Journalism Club got busy producing the second edition of *Shedders* magazine. After the first edition only broke even, they decided not to print the July 2010 edition of *Shedders*. It was only available online through Mag Cloud. The girls knew their business needed to continue to evolve if it was ever going to be an income generator for them and the school.

Meanwhile, a teacher in San Diego named Steve Le contacted them about joining his young writing students in a new chapter of the Global Journalism Project. KGSA students submitted articles and poems, which the Global Journalism Project published alongside pieces from students in San Diego. They mailed KGSA 100 copies of each magazine so the girls could see their names in print, and a strong cross-cultural writing community was formed. To this day, students in San Diego and Kibera are in touch over social media because of the project. The girls' voices were being heard.

Anne Baldwin, who taught physics at KGSA in 2008, returned in June with a $10,000 Davis Project for Peace Grant. She planned to work for peace by giving the KGSA students skills to fight economic violence. "Promoting gender equality is promoting peace," she said.

She partnered with Sandy Wycliffe, a man who worked in Kibera regularly, to run a three-day workshop on how to make solar-powered light bulbs. The first day, the girls learned about the negative effects of kerosene and the environmental advantages to using solar power.

The second day, the girls learned about circuits and electricity. The third day, the girls walked into the laboratory ready to build their first solar lamps. All the materials were laid out on newspapers at stations. They spent the day soldering their solar lamps and cell phone chargers. Abdul walked around amazed. Neighbors poked their heads in to see what was happening. The girls took their work very seriously.

Violet was the star of the workshops. She came early in a NASCAR jersey with her hair done up. She looked so mature without her KGSA uniform that Anne barely recognized her. "Violet was regal. She was quiet without being quiet, like she had an inner stillness. I had a friend-crush on Violet," Anne laughed.

Violet sat up front during the lectures and kept the other girls focused. When it was time to build, she was the first one finished. She ran outside to test it, holding the lamp up to the sun in the middle of the courtyard. Her face was filled with hope and excitement. It worked. When it lit up, Violet laughed aloud before realizing Anne was watching her. A little embarrassed at her own joy, she straightened up and rushed back into the lab to help the other girls finish their lamps.

In the end, all the girls got their solar lamps to work. They were so proud, and for awhile at KGSA, it was cool to do physics and have your own solar lamp.

The Physics Club came up with a checkout system for the KGSA students who needed lamps to study at night. During class, the lamps hung outside the classroom charging. They quickly became a hot commodity, so the club started thinking about how to expand the project.

The informal markets swelling from the slums are driven by creativity, entrepreneurship, and the need to survive. A small amount of knowledge or skill can catapult a person ahead in the market. The girls saw the solar light bulbs as a way to turn knowledge and skills into capital. "Could we sell them? How much would Kiberans be willing to pay? Is renting them more realistic?" they wondered.

If they kept the chargers at KGSA, renters might have more incentive to return the lamps instead of stealing them. They become useless when they run out of juice.

A girl named Cynthia was named president of the Solar Club. In primary school, math was Cynthia's favorite subject. At KGSA, she fell in love with physics. Cynthia decided she wanted to become a civil engineer. She loved learning. When she was admitted to KGSA, she smiled through her whole first day of class. She smiled during the entire walk home.

"I had never seen girls with so much hope and oomph; they were, and still are, so determined to succeed. Just watching the teachers teach inspired me. I never thought I would go to high school, and there I was sitting and writing notes from the chalkboard, raising my hand when I had a question or wanted to answer any question in class. I just fell in love with school. I loved the feeling of having education."

Anne, as a professional female scientist, inspired Cynthia. She told Anne that they wanted to find more ways to bring electricity to people in Kibera who could not afford it. "I love using the sun to produce light for people. I'm going to implement what I was taught in school, to learn and believe in myself, to be focused and know my rights as a woman."

Before making surplus lamps to sell in Kibera, the girls found a comparable product coming out of India that was selling for cheaper than KGSA could sell them. So Anne used the rest of her grant money to buy that product and put her efforts into teaching the club how to market and sell them for profit.

Anne said, "The Solar Club was making the business decisions, not me. We broke them up into three committees: the engineers, the marketers, and the sales associates. My hope was that some of the girls would get into it and see how these skills could lead to a good job as an electrician. They need to apprentice people to gain more skills and confidence. I wish I could have stayed longer to make sure the Solar Club was healthy, but I had to go."

In October, Anne had brought a businessman into Kibera to talk to the girls. He had a backpack with a laptop, Blackberry, passport, and camera in it. As she was walking him out, a path she took every day, four men surrounded them. A man with a gun tore Anne's necklace off, pointed the gun at her face, and started choking her with his free hand while the other three robbed the man. The gunman pushed Anne to the ground, shoved her face in the dirt, put the gun to the back of her head, and said, "Say goodbye."

Then the four men took off running with the stolen backpack.

The girls didn't understand why Anne felt the need to leave. Trying to get her to stay, they told her stories of worse things that had happened to them. "He didn't kill you. They just stole your things. This happens to us all the time. It's okay," they said.

For Anne, it wasn't okay. She was worn thin, and this was the last straw. She took a week to orient another KGSA teacher to lead the Solar Club, making business introductions and handing over a packet documenting the progress of the club. Then she went home.

Over the previous few years, Omparkash had been a strategic, supportive vehicle for the KGSA Foundation. They funneled money from the United States to the school. They gave MSID volunteer Jake Naughton a grant to shoot a video about water in Kibera. The film raised enough funds to build a clean water station at the school. They sent two American volunteers, Claire and Caroline, to KGSA for a summer. Claire and Caroline worked with a poet named Pepe to get the girls to participate in poetry performances and competitions in downtown Nairobi. They trained them on interviewing skills for *Shedders* and got them tested for HIV. They ran kickboxing, sex education, and self-defense classes. However, Ryan was eager to get the KGSA Foundation to be independent, and his work paid off.

He got a call from his contact in legal filings. "Ryan, I just want to give you a heads up that your application has been received and approved by the IRS." The KGSA Foundation had its 501(c)3 status. It was a relief for KGSA to be its own entity. Teka and Abdul had access to the account. The money was tax-deductible.

To celebrate, Ryan threw a launch party at an Irish pub in downtown Minneapolis when the KGSA episode of "On the Road with Jason Davis" aired. Ryan had brought Jason Davis, a local reporter, to Kibera to film an episode of his travel show. Jason told Ryan it was the best episode he had ever done.

Ryan stood among his friends and family, officially the director of the KGSA Foundation. He ordered Tuskers, Kenyan lagers, all night. He cried silently through the whole television show as Abdul's and the girls' faces were projected on a big screen in the bar. The party raised $4,000, the first official donation to the KGSA Foundation.

The money continued to come in slowly. Ryan quickly realized that it's hard to make Americans care, to ask people for money in a world of skeptics and donor fatigue. It was hard to compete with big foundations that have marketing teams and use emotional manipulation to get a buck. Abdul believed that sustainable partnerships could only be built with people who have come to KGSA to see the school for themselves. Ryan told the story to people who did not have the means to fly to Kenya. He asked them to trust him, to support the school until it was strong enough to run itself. It was a hard sell.

Donors in the U.S. wanted to see measured success, but Abdul saw success in areas that are hard to measure. KGSA was not sending many students to college. Test scores were improving more slowly than KGSA would like, but they were seeing success in the confidence of the students and the marketable skills the girls were gaining through the clubs. KGSA had made progress for girls in grades six, seven, and eight. It had given them hope that there could be another four years of school—that there was a place that values women. It was hard to show donors that the girls' sense of self-worth was improving, but that was more important than test scores to Abdul.

It was a challenging, low-paying gig for Ryan. Getting paid $650 a month, Ryan lived with his father to cut costs. "Money was always tight, but it's so hard to raise money for my own salary when I know the money should be going to support the school."

Ryan raised money for the school and helped Abdul make connections and contacts. It was a daily dance of balancing immediate needs against building sustainability. Knowing which individuals and organizations in which to invest time is often purely instinctual. Ryan and Abdul came together across age, race, ethnicity, and religious lines to reach consensus. Abdul was a busy man doing important work. It took courage for Ryan to ask him to work even harder. Ryan admired Abdul so much, it was hard to know when and how to push.

For example, Ryan planned a meeting with Kennedy Odede, a Kiberan who was a big name in the development world. He wanted Abdul to meet this man and start networking. But Abdul didn't show up. Ryan called and texted, but he ended up going to the meeting by himself without Abdul. Abdul had double-booked himself and was at a grade school helping them relocate to a safer space. If he could help it, however, Ryan never wanted to be the only representative of KGSA in an important meeting—especially with a big player like Kennedy.

The subtext was, as it often was between these two, "Abdul, I know you are so busy and give so much. I know you have done amazing things. And I know I may have no right to an opinion. But I think this is really big. This connection will help me build the foundation. Please trust me. Please follow through." Almost always, Abdul did.

The uphill battle continued. Ryan found the nonprofit world unexpectedly competitive and subject to corruption and miscommunication. Robison Rider, the American who helped Abdul and Salim coach Girls Soccer in Kibera, formed his own 501(c)3 called Girls Soccer in Kibera. He had a separate board and a separate website, but he also used the story and pictures of KGSA to raise money. This was confusing to donors.

Initially, Robison had provided some great capital to the soccer program at KGSA. When Jamie, Shaun, and Ryan were first discussing the possibility of making a nonprofit, Abdul suggested they partner with Robison. They reached out, but Robison wasn't interested in working with the MSID students. Over time, Salim, who was getting all the money from Robison funneled through him, quit KGSA and moved out of Kibera. The money funneled through Salim stopped getting to the school. The last donation Abdul saw was $200 that Robison gave in 2006, the very first year of the school.

Robison was unaware that Salim was stealing the money. When it became clear to Abdul that the KGSA Foundation, with Ryan as director, was going to be the main vehicle in the United States to funnel money to the school, he confronted Robison, asking him to join forces with Ryan. Robison had not been to Kenya in two years, and when he came to visit, Salim admitted that he had not been a part of the school and that the school was not benefiting from Robison's fundraising.

Abdul told Robison, "If you want to be a part of this, you need to be a part of the KGSA Foundation. You need to give money to the school and not Salim. He can't be trusted with donors' money."

Abdul chose the KGSA Foundation over Girls Soccer in Kibera and made the break from Salim official. Robison and Ryan were at odds in the United States, for years running separate 501(c)3s that raised money for Kibera. Ryan gave his money to Abdul and Robison gave his to Salim.

The KGSA Foundation's business model hinged on the fact that Abdul could be trusted with money. What made him different from other men who might intercept donor money instead of funneling it into the community? His answer was simple.

"One thing I know. The girls will come to me. They will take the packet of *ugali* that I had for my family. If everybody else at KGSA walks out on me, it is still going to be my problem. The girls won't walk away. They will still come asking me for help. So getting this support, this money, is first and foremost helping me. Now that we have support from France, Holland, the U.K., and the U.S., I don't have to dig deep into my pocket all of the time like I used to for the girls. These kids, you cannot wish them away. Unlike a lot of organizations, we are hands-on at KGSA. We have these kids here every day. I would have shot myself in the foot if I spent the money on me. I look at it as me being relieved. I see the supported school really blossoming in the girls. That is more rewarding than having the money for myself.

"Also, I worked for Telkom for twenty years. I have always worked for my own money. I get it. I earn it. I work within a budget. Now and then, I have a few extra shillings. On my own, I'm fairly comfortable. There is no reason to put my hand into the till. If I need more money, I can talk to Ryan and I will get it.

"At first, I helped the girls with my own money because I could. There were so few of them. I knew that if I didn't, someone else would help, for a price. That is when they'd get pregnant. Now, there are so many girls, I need the donations to get them stable.

"I've never thought about using money to leave Kibera. I get a fair amount of salary, and, yeah, I could easily get a house somewhere outside, but that has never crossed my mind. It would be like running from a purpose. We have come all this way. My home is here, my work is here."

Can KGSA survive without Abdul? Is this model sustainable if there is no one else like Abdul in the world? For the KGSA Foundation to continue assuring donors that their money is going toward the needs of the girls at KGSA, Abdul's successor also has to be trustworthy with money. Teka may be that person. In the beginning, Teka was Abdul's sidekick. Abdul seemed larger than life, and Teka followed in his wake, comfortable to be in his shadow.

It quickly became more nuanced. Teka, at KGSA all day, every day, knew the name of every student and had an exciting vision for the school. Abdul was the public face of the school and tended to the surrounding family. He was strengthening the school by looking at how the parents and the primary schools were doing. Meanwhile, Teka was driving the daily operation. He emerged from the role of sidekick, and he knew it.

"Before I joined Girls Soccer," Teka said, "I had never come into contact with any *mzungu*, any white man. I used to think that white people were very special people, maybe closer to God. If I saw an African talking to a white man, I used to think the African was very special because he was talking to a white man. I thought it was impossible for me to be friends with white people.

"I used to be nervous and timid around Shaun, Ryan, and Jamie. I thanked Abdul because he was at Telkom full-time and so I had to take over. I had to learn to deal with white people in order to get funding for the school. KGSA finally got support from Kenyans, but at first it was only *mzungus*.

"I didn't learn in university. I learned through experience. I felt like I could come up with a project, defend it, and get money for it. That is a skill.

"Many times, when we got grant money, we had to be trained on implementing and reporting. The donors were helpful. They couldn't always just give money to the people who know everything. They gave us money and taught us what we needed to know to manage it. They taught us how to report so they didn't have to pull out of the projects. Then I had confidence in finding funding for the school. It was exciting."

KGSA needed Abdul in the beginning. Part of his brilliance, though, was in supporting the whole family, students and teachers, interns and volunteers. He never knew who, with a little stability, would become the new hero.

To take the KCSE exam, the girls needed to present their birth certificates, which was sometimes a problem. Birth certificates got lost in the move from rural Kenya to Kibera, and many people lost documents during the postelection violence. Violet's birth certificate was in her rural home, and she didn't have enough money to travel there to look for it. She kept her worries to herself as the test day approached until Teka finally asked her what was wrong.

"I can't afford to go to my village to get my birth certificate."

"How much is your bus fare from Nairobi to the rural place?"

"Two thousand shillings."

Teka gave her the money, just like that. She was stunned, but she took it gratefully. When Violet returned with the certificate and knew she could take the test, she was giddy at school.

"Violet, have you found the birth certificate?" Teka asked.

"Yeah."

"Okay, that is why you are so happy today."

Teka told the girls before the exam, "Take good care. This one will determine who you will be in the future. Don't panic."

Violet thought, "When they say don't panic, of course we were panicking. We had to handle it carefully. We miss, we destroy our futures."

Linet had even more at stake than Violet. She had been made fun of all year for being a "repeater." But on the brink of her second KCSE, she had the advantage of knowing what to expect. She felt more comfortable the second time, in part because she could take it at KGSA and feel at home.

Ida walked into her KCSE exam brimming with confidence. Her father had not supported her getting an education at KGSA. He thought only his sons would go beyond primary school. She wanted to prove her worth to him by not only graduating, but going on to college. She was at the top of her class with Violet and Linet, and she had big dreams to fulfill.

Some of the very first students at KGSA never dreamed of attending secondary school; going to KGSA was a dream come true. Graduating was the goal. Ida exemplified the growth of KGSA in just one year. She set her goals high and was vocal about them.

She not only wanted to take the test, she wanted to pass it, and pass it well. Other girls in her class also started dreaming of post-secondary school.

A week before the KCSE exam, Asha asked Ida, "Do you think you are going to perform well?"

She said, "What kind of question are you asking? That is already a reality. I am going to perform. I am going to get a B."

B was the magic grade that brought the possibility of a government scholarship for college.

Hopes were high in the 2010 graduating class, yet there were still so many obstacles. Many of the girls lived in unstable homes. Breakfast and dinner were not a guarantee. No electricity, no privacy, and chores like fetching water and cooking food made it hard to study at night. Teachers at KGSA, who were still getting paid only 7,000 shillings, about eighty U.S. dollars, per month would come and go, making it hard to build consistency in the classroom. Most of the teachers had not been to college themselves. Girls growing up in Kibera were told that they did not deserve to go to college. Their path was to marry early, stay home, and have children. It was thought that education was not required for these tasks. The KGSA girls started believing that they could wait to marry. They dreamed together of a different path, going to school, getting jobs, and supporting themselves. Yet their economic situation and the educational structure in Kenya worked against them.

KGSA hosted the KCSE for the twenty-five fourth-year students graduating in 2010. They hoped the home-court advantage would make a difference. Violet, Linet, and Ida took the exam in November, graduated from KGSA in December, and waited for their results. Results could take up to four months to come out, and if they did get their Bs, they couldn't start attending college until January of 2012. In Kenya, they call this "the year of waiting." Starehe Girls' School offers a fifth year while students wait to begin college. For KGSA graduates, a year of waiting passively is dangerous. The free KGSA lunch stopped abruptly at graduation. They needed to eat, so they needed to work.

Violet explained, "It doesn't do to just sit around the house. I needed pants. I needed pads. And I couldn't go to boys to get money. I couldn't risk pregnancy or diseases. I finished fourth year. The results were coming out in March. Could I just wait while my mother went out looking for a little sum for us both? No. I chose work."

She found work as house help that paid 200 shillings, about two U.S. dollars, per day. She woke at 5:00 a.m., started walking by 5:30, and arrived at the house in a wealthier neighborhood by 8:00. She worked there for three weeks until she wasn't needed anymore.

"I was lucky. I stayed at home only two days before I got another job tutoring a little boy. It also paid 200 shillings a day."

Then the KCSE results came out. Seventeen of the twenty-five girls passed the KCSE with a D or above. Five of the students reached the C− mark that allows applications to diploma programs. For the first time, KGSA was sending students to the next level.

Ida didn't get her B. She didn't score high enough to get a college scholarship.

"I was one of the best in my class, so I always thought I would make it. My teachers helped me believe it. In high school, I dreamt of a lot of things. But once I stepped away from that school, once I was out of that uniform and tie, all the dreams evaporated. So what comes next is a job. I'm a hustler. I don't make wages that help me live a life. I'm teaching in primary school and my new dream is just to be a high school teacher.

"If you asked me, 'Ida, what do you want to be when you grow up?' I used to dream that I would be the first woman president of Kenya. I believed it! But those were just dreams. To be a teacher, we call it plan B. My life is plan B. Just like that, just because of the exam. Because I don't have a degree, I will never be paid much. I think it is cruel that they let us dream like that at KGSA. When I said I wanted to be president, they should have told me to be ready for plan B. The exam is just too much, too cruel."

In her pain, she directed her confusion and anger at KGSA. Asha, then a third-year student, was watching.

"After four years of big dreams, she had nothing. From that day on, I never saw her in school. She blamed KGSA and thought she was a failure. She was head girl, a great soccer player, the president of Journalism Club. If she could not do it, how could I dream of college?"

Violet, on the other hand, was not devastated but hopeful. "I got a C. With this C, I can go to college. Now where do we get the money for tuition?"

Linet, on her second try, improved. In Swahili and English, her scores went from a C− to a C+, which brought her composite score up significantly.

"I was so excited that repeating paid off. But I didn't even have the registration money required to apply to university, let alone the tuition to go if I got in. Josephat had gotten into school, so I had to be the one to make money for us. I found a job teaching small children in school. Now and then, they would give me 500 shillings. Not all children can speak Swahili, only their tribal languages. We came to understand each other and it was fun."

For the first time, KGSA graduates were looking to go on to post-secondary education, and Abdul needed to decide if KGSA would play a role in their next steps. His school had planted the seeds and nurtured the desires, but it was not yet equipped to financially expand beyond offering free secondary school. Five students, including Violet and Linet, stood by, waiting.

Abdul and Ryan expected more and more students to get a passing grade on the KCSE each year, so the precedent was important. These girls see college in life-and-death terms, so Ryan didn't want to promise that the foundation could send every student who passed to college without being able to follow through. He also needed to keep supporting the existing school and the existing students; that is the foundation's primary mission. But how could he tell these girls they couldn't go to college?

It costs about U.S. $1,500 to send a student to college for a year in Kenya. To families paying $50,000 a year in the U.S., this may seem like nothing. To the girls from Kibera, it is an amount they can barely fathom. For a young foundation that frequently deals in much smaller sums, it was a reach, but it also felt like too important a dream to abandon.

THRIVING GIRLS CHANGE THE WORLD
2011

A person is a person through other people.
—DESMOND TUTU

A KGSA soccer game one Sunday was supposed to start at ten. Teka showed up an hour late after church. With him was a man with a plastic bag with two beat-up soccer balls. "Neither team brought a ball to the game. So I had to go borrow balls from this guy. He thought I was going to steal them, so he came with me as collateral."

The game started when the soccer balls arrived. None of this fazed anyone. Spectators sat on the dry grass under trees on the sidelines by Kibera Girls Soccer. The goals didn't have nets, and the grass wasn't marked.

Kibera Girls scored within the first thirty seconds. They were very athletic and well trained, passing and ball-handling easily around their opponents. These young women were exhilarating to watch. They controlled the ball and pace of the game. They were fearless and precise.

Toward the middle of the second half, Coach Byrones made three substitutions. As the girls were running off the field, they started taking off their jerseys. They handed the shirts to the girls waiting to go in. The team had only eleven jerseys, just enough for the girls playing. One girl even took off her cleats and handed them over to her replacement, who was waiting in socks to join the game.

By the end of the game, the initial number of spectators had almost doubled, most of them men. After the struggle the girls went through to gain respect as athletes, it was exciting that men were supporting girls' soccer. The girls were changing Kibera one game at a time. After a few short years, it no longer seemed strange that girls were playing soccer or that men were coming to watch them win. The coaches were men. The official was a man. Where were the other women? Where were these players' friends? They were making food and washing clothes, caring for small children and going to church, praying for a break in life. KGSA would not feel that its work was done until women are also the coaches, officials, and spectators on the sidelines.

The score remained 1-0, and for Coach Byrones, a win was not enough. "We should have scored more goals," Coach Byrones said. "The girls relaxed as soon as they scored."

At the end of the game, Teka gave the man back his two soccer balls and gave Coach Byrones money for the girls' lunch. Providing lunch was the only way to guarantee that the team ate.

The conversations that took place at KGSA often centered on the importance of free education, of delaying pregnancy and early marriage, of eliminating child prostitution and eradicating poverty. But the school also carved out time and space for these girls to run and kick, to be in their bodies as powerful athletes, to be free. The girls spent a Sunday afternoon playing soccer in the warm sun—running, sweating, yelling, laughing, and playing. In Kibera, that is nothing short of revolutionary.

In Kibera and all over the world, something ugly happens to girls in adolescent years, for which sports is a healthy corrective. Girls think being feminine means being cute and catty. They show up timid and lazy. Then they learn the dignity of hard work, sweat, and putting the team above the win. They set goals and work incrementally to achieve them in a space where boys are not allowed. They develop a work ethic and an identity that will be a part of them for the rest of their lives. They finally see that muscles are beautiful, and that family is, in fact, the only win there is. They realize, "I kick serious ass. If I can do this, I can do anything."

When talking about a big soccer win, the KGSA players involuntarily sat up straighter, talked louder, got excited, and lost themselves in the memory of the moment. The soccer field was, for them, a battleground where they were fighting for their freedom. The field was a tangible space where girls could use their bodies to struggle against the oppression and break through it to find another way of being. The players used soccer as a metaphor, an allegory, for their struggles off the field. Every loss, every practice, had something to teach about life. Soccer helped them believe they were strong, equal, and powerful and that their liberation started in their own bodies. They were, indeed, agents in their own transformation.

A successful soccer team went out and founded a successful school; in hindsight, it made perfect sense that a school made up of soccer teammates and headed by its coach turned into a family. Even years later, when only a fraction of the students played soccer competitively, the school felt like one big, healthy team working toward victory. The school was more than soccer, but soccer was an undeniable key to its success.

The head soccer coach Byrones embodied and promoted the strategic crossover between KGSA the school and KGSA the soccer team. He could have just shown up at the field for games, but instead he spent a lot of time at the school. He came in during the late morning in jeans and a track jacket, checked his email in the library, arranged logistics for food and transportation, and talked to the girls during their breaks. He understood that he was not just coaching soccer. Byrones wanted to know how his players were doing at school and at home. Improving their game was most important as a tool for improving their lives.

Byrones first saw Girls Soccer in Kibera play way back in 2004 before the school existed. He knew right away that something special was going on. "They were pretty young, they looked very ambitious, they had the desire to play. You can't coach that, that desire. They just had it. I could see it in their eyes."

Salim, Abdul's former partner, brought Byrones into the fold to teach. Abdul remembered, "The girls were behind in Byrones's class. He was being lazy. When I approached him about being behind in the syllabus, he lied to me. So I fired him."

Byrones's fiancée had left him. He lost weight. He kept coming around, clearly missing KGSA. Byrones apologized. Abdul was protective of the classroom, but invited him to be part of the soccer staff. Bryones was a great player in his own right, but not yet a great coach. He took courses, developed curriculum, and was running the program by 2011.

Byrones used the Socratic method when coaching. He didn't yell, but rather asked questions. "'What do you think you should have done there? When do you think you should have executed a shot?' Then they give the right answer. 'So why didn't you?' So often they say, 'I didn't believe in myself, I wasn't sure it would go in.'"

He loved seeing potential in girls that they didn't see themselves.

"At times a player will tell me, 'I think I'm comfortable playing defense.' But in their strengths and abilities, I see a striker. I tell her she is a striker, and she looks at me like I'm crazy. Then I keep on pushing and after a game or two it works, and she thinks, 'Ah, I am the best striker in the world!'"

KGSA was playing in the semifinal in a tournament in Nairobi. The agreement was that the organizers of the tournament would pay for transportation for KGSA. The night before the game, the money hadn't come through. Byrones called in the morning, but by that time, he knew they would not get to the field in time and they would lose by default.

The organizers decided, "No, this is a semifinal match, and there is no way we are awarding a bye."

They sent a bus, and the girls had to change en route. Byrones knew they would get to the field cold, tight, and rushed. He was right. Their opponents scored within the first twenty minutes. KGSA was being outplayed.

At half time, Byrones said, "Ladies, we've come a long way to just be beaten. We are humble from Kibera, yes, but that doesn't make us timid. Everybody is thinking, 'You cannot do it, because you are from Kibera.' But we can get back into this game. They had their half. They scored their goal. And now we are warm. It's our turn. Let's win this game."

Within five minutes of the second half, KGSA got a free kick outside the penalty area. Rose arched the ball into the net. The noisy crowd went quiet.

Byrones imagined everybody thinking, "Ah, so the girls from Kibera can play."

He was thinking, "Yes, shut up and watch my girls play."

KGSA controlled the play and the clock the second half, keeping the ball on the opponent's side. When they got another free kick, Byrones made Rose take it again just in case people thought her first shot was lucky.

"She took it and, yes, a second goal. That goal got us a lot of publicity. Everybody wanted to talk to this Rose from Kibera. There were clubs that had buses and great facilities and pay their players allowances. We don't have money, but we won. I have orphans and kids from single parents on my team. I am an orphan too. I tell my girls, 'People should not look at your face and tell that you're an orphan. Don't feel sorry for yourself, be intimidated, or withdraw. Stick out your neck and say, yes, I am an orphan, but I am here to play.'"

KGSA offered free lunch to the players. Most players didn't have three square meals a day. Byrones wished he could offer more, like nice facilities or a stipend.

The KGSA team was not like high school teams in the United States. Most of the players on the team also went to KGSA for school, though it was not a requirement. KGSA had ten and under, twelve and under, fourteen and under, sixteen and under, eighteen and under, and seniors teams. The players on the junior teams were encouraged to go to KGSA for secondary, but they were not coerced. On the eighteen and under team, which was most like a secondary school team, there were twenty-two players. Twelve of the twenty-two went to KGSA. Additionally, graduates and former students who didn't graduate could keep playing. Some of Byrones's main players were the breadwinners for their families. He realized the sacrifices they were making to continue to play.

Byrones encouraged girls to play no matter what their age or ability. He could see how soccer helped these girls and young women demand that men treat them with respect. "It's not about competition; it's about how soccer makes them fit into society. It's not about winning the league, but learning self-discipline and life skills. Soccer is a strength that will keep them independent and safe."

For the players who did go to KGSA, he made home visits to see their living situations and encourage their studies.

"The visits get them to understand that we care about more than just soccer. Education is a pillar. They will get derailed and lose their way without it. We need to create bridges to employment. Soccer for ladies is not very commercial. It will be hard for them to play for money. They need to know I am watching, and I am concerned. Players are always a reflection of the coach. If I don't have disciplined players, if they are unruly and uncouth, that points to the coach. I want it to be our philosophy in the whole program: humble, disciplined, educated."

When players decided to leave, he encouraged them to stay in the program as mentors.

"We want all female coaches, officials, and players to take over and champion the program. They can carry the philosophy to the next level. These are the women who will take my job from me, and that is how it should be. Our little girls should have female coaches they can look up to and hope to be like someday."

Byrones knew how to make soccer about so much more than soccer. The program, backed by his philosophy, benefited each player in her own right. Once you were on the team, you were family. So many of the players needed that sense of belonging. Take, for example, the story of two sisters and teammates, Josephine and Maureen. Josephine may be one of those girls who will take over the soccer program from Byrones someday. She was mature, a natural mentor to younger girls, and she understood the game. Even in her uniform skirt, Josephine looked like an athlete. She wore her hair in tight braids and had defined calf muscles under her uniform socks. She was quiet and serious, very serious. Even when she smiled, her eyes never lost focus. She was focused about school and soccer. There was a kindness, a deep gentleness in her spirit. But it was as if she could see the next goal in a space somewhere between you and her, and she never took her eye off that spot. She nodded calmly. She knew she'd get there.

Josephine was raised in the Rift Valley with her younger adopted sister, Maureen. Their mother divorced their father and left them to move to Nairobi. Josephine and Maureen were very close to their father, who raised them well. They went through primary school in the Rift Valley Province, which is where they fell in love with soccer. Their school valued sports and required them to play on a daily basis.

While Josephine and Maureen were still in primary school, their father died. Their mother came to the funeral, and Josephine asked her to take them with her to Nairobi.

"I knew it would be hard to get to know her a second time. She left us when we were very little, but with her in Kibera, we were happy and felt loved. I finished my primary school and went to a secondary school."

Josephine's mother also got sick and had to stop working. Her brothers made enough to feed the girls, but Josephine dropped out of secondary school and took care of her mother. She didn't improve.

The family decided to take her back to her rural home in hopes that the fresh air outside the slum would help her. They left Maureen alone in Kibera to guard the house and keep going to school as a first-year student at KGSA. They talked to the neighbors and asked them to keep a good eye on Maureen. Josephine got on a bus with her brothers and her mother, praying that her mother would recover.

"She died on our way to the rural village," Josephine said. "I watched her die. First my father, then my mother. We arrived at the village with a corpse. It was as if she wanted to die in her village."

They sent word back to Maureen in Kibera. Teka, Byrones, and a few of the girls accompanied Maureen to the funeral. Josephine couldn't believe that the KGSA community came so far to offer support.

"That gave us strength. After the funeral, my parents' family wanted to separate us and take each one of us to different houses. We refused and said that we would be fine in Kibera."

Maureen wanted to stay at KGSA. "I loved how passionate the girls at KGSA were about school. When the teachers came to class, the atmosphere changed from jokes to seriousness. I loved the way the students answered questions and how the teachers involved the students in discussions."

Josephine and Maureen's brothers continued to support them with living expenses. KGSA offered to pay their rent and food so that Maureen and Josephine could keep on studying.

"Byrones showed unwavering support when we were grieving for my mother," Josephine said. "He told me I could come to KGSA too, and I agreed without any hesitation. Maybe it was going to be the family I had always wanted. My first day was very exciting because the school felt warm. The girls had smiles that never faded. After class, the coach told me to go to trainings and games. I was so excited because I was going to play on the same team as my sister. The soccer team is like a family."

Maureen, unlike most girls as talented at soccer as she was, didn't know if she wanted to be a soccer player when she graduated. She wanted to be an artist because she said she felt at home when she drew. "I want to know how to invest my money, and I don't want soccer managers to manipulate me. If I get an education, then I will get money and not need men who will use me. I am a very talented girl, and I plan to use my knowledge for the good of the community."

One day, Abdul called Rose and asked, "Where are you?"

"I'm plaiting hair, and I can't leave."

"You have to come to selection right now. You'll make it."

They were making selections for the 2011 Homeless World Cup, which is a four-on-four small-arena soccer tournament. It's a quick game. Kenya had never sent a women's team before. The 2011 tournament was held in Paris. Rose didn't go to tryouts right away, because she didn't think she had a shot. She was the thirtieth woman on the field, and they selected only eight women.

The training was rigorous in more ways than one. It was a trek from Kibera, requiring Rose to wake up early and take multiple buses with no fare provided. There was no lunch offered as at KGSA practice. It was a huge time and financial risk, with no payoff if she was one of the twenty-two ladies cut. Abdul pushed her to keep going.

"Don't give up. You're supposed to do it."

"I don't see it. I don't know. The coaches are harsh. When I do my best, they don't encourage me. The way is long and expensive. I'm getting out."

She dropped out after two weeks of tryouts, but the man in charge called Abdul, saying that he wanted her back on the field.

"You used to dream of getting on an airplane when you were little, Rose," Abdul pleaded. "This is it. This is your shot."

After a few more days of training, they had thinned the field from thirty to nine. Then they discovered that one of the women was not, in fact, poor. By checking her Facebook page, they found out she had been outside of the country twice. She was cut, and Rose was going to Paris to represent Kenya in the 2011 Homeless World Cup.

Commando made the team too. After growing up together, going to KGSA together, and playing on the same field for years, Rose and Commando were roommates in Paris. They supported each other throughout the adventure, proud that two of the eight team members were representing Kibera and KGSA.

Rose had never been on an airplane before. She held a hand to her heart as she looked out the window, not believing how high up they were. She didn't want to sleep on the long flight, because she didn't want to miss anything. She loved that she could watch any movie she wanted on the screen in front of her.

When she got to the grounds of the tournament, the rumor was that Brazil and Mexico were the teams to beat. The Kenyan ladies were intimidated, but they told each other: "They have two legs. We have two legs. Let's go and play."

Kenya did not play in the first day of pool play, so they watched Brazil win 3-0. The defending champions were, it seemed, the team to beat.

France was Kenya's first opponent on day two. In small-arena four-on-four competition, one woman stayed in the goal the whole game and two groups of three each played a half in the field. Rose and Commando, having so much experience together, were put in the same group of three and played the second half. They said, "We're going to beat France in their own country." And they did. Kenya won 4-0. They proceeded to beat the Netherlands, the United States, and England. Kenya was turning heads. Their only loss in pool play was to Mexico, and the score was a close 4-3.

After a quarterfinal win, Kenya had the attention of the reporters. They were set to meet Brazil in the semifinals. Kenya beat Brazil in the semifinal match 4-3, making history. To win the finals, they would have to beat Mexico, the team that beat them in pool play.

Both Kenya and Mexico played well. By the end of the game, it was tied 3-3. In penalty kicks, Rose kicked the deciding goal. Kenya beat Mexico to take home the 2011 Homeless World Cup. It was their first trip to the tournament.

"I was so proud I cried," Rose said simply.

Rose felt at home in the soccer arena, but the rest of the experience was a bit daunting. Kenyans living in France came to cheer them on. They took the girls on boat rides and to museums. They went shopping for nice clothes. The friends that Commando and Rose made from the Netherlands offered to help them escape. It hadn't ever crossed their minds.

"We had to go back home. I was homesick. I thought about my daughter, whom I left to play soccer even though she should be breast-feeding. We were missing Kenyan food so much. I wanted to be back in Kenya. I didn't have Facebook or an email address. So I have never heard from my friends from the Netherlands again."

The Kenyan women came home with two silver plates and a gold cup. When they got to the airport, reporters asked them a few questions and then left. The wife of the head of Kenyan football was there to pick him up, and they left with the trophy. Rose never saw him or the trophy again. Rose and Commando looked at each other in shock. They had not lined up a ride home, assuming one would be provided. They had no money. They had no way to get home.

"If we went to the Homeless World Cup, how did they think we could afford to get home from the airport? Where was our welcome party? They know that we are champions. But they are not taking care of us. It felt bad, but what could we do? We have to go on, after all."

The girls found an employee who let them use his phone to call their coach. They waited quietly to get picked up.

Rose had sacrificed so much to train and play in the tournament. They had been promised money if they won, but they received nothing. She was disappointed, but she did not lose sight of her dream to play professionally and support her family through soccer.

"Soccer is my talent. I can't turn my back on it. If I made it in France, why not in Kenya? I just hope God will give me a chance. I thought things would be different when I came back, but I was wrong. I'm going to try for the under-twenty-three national team. I will make it. I will make it."

All of Kibera cheers for girls like Rose as they train to become serious contenders on the Kenyan national soccer stage. It's remarkable that a girl who started playing with a ball made of trash and string got to play and win in Paris after having a baby. But that accomplishment, sadly, does not equate with making it. Being named to the national team might not mean making it either. Rose will, realistically speaking, need to be spotted by teams in Europe or the Americas to get paid a living wage to play soccer.

The year 2011 was full of success on the soccer field and in the classroom. Three graduates—Violet, Linet, and Irene—started postsecondary classes, and several from the graduating class of 2011 would become eligible to apply.

Violet got a C on her KCSE exam, and Teka called her with good news.

"I found a sponsor who is willing to send you to college."

"That's great! When can I start?"

"We need to wait for the money to come through, but in the meantime, come work as an accountant at the school. You are good at math. You are starting work tomorrow."

"Going to work with my teachers, eating with them? Wow!" she laughed.

She went to KGSA the next day at 8:00 a.m. and found a pile of receipts waiting for her. By noon they were filed.

"Teka told me, 'You are such a hardworking girl.' Of course! As a working woman, I can get soap. I know I can feed myself."

The students knew she was good at math and asked her for help during breaks.

"Yeah, I can assist you. I have come to give back to the community. It's four years. Dedicate yourself."

The Kenya Community Development Fund (KCDF) was the organization sponsoring Violet's education. As soon as the money came through, she traveled downtown to look at colleges, compare tuitions, and apply. She decided to attend Nairobi Institute of Business

Studies (NIBS). She took her money to the principal of NIBS and said, "When can I start learning? I am eager."

He told her, "Even today."

Back at KGSA, after filing the receipt for her tuition, she realized that she had no supplies. "Mr. Teka, can you give me a book and a pen?" she asked. "I'm starting classes today."

"How is it that you are starting so early?"

"I have to learn. When God has blessed you with an opportunity, use it wisely. Don't let it escape."

She was the youngest in her courses by far. At first, she was intimidated, but eventually she started talking to her older classmates. It had been a while since she had attended school with men. She realized she was savvier with technology than her classmates, which put her at an advantage. She taught her classmates how to use their calculators and became an instant hit. "You are young, but you are great," they laughed.

Violet worked at KGSA during the day and went to class at night and on the weekends. She took one course at a time, and when she passed the exam, she was able to go on to the next course. If she didn't, she had to take the course again. Her first exam consisted of five tests that took three days to complete, and then she waited a month for her results. She had to score above 50 percent to move on.

She continued as the assistant accountant at KGSA and waited nervously.

Then she received a message from the examination board: "Violet, you have earned five credits. Pass, pass, pass, pass, pass."

Excited, she went back to the principal that same day to register for the next course. "I passed! I'm starting immediately. Today."

She made steady progress and seemed hopeful. "I thank KGSA for what they did for me. I want to be an accountant. I want to work in a major firm and at KGSA. I'm training very hard and saving a little. [Once I have] 20,000 shillings, I can buy iron sheets and build a small house.

"Once I started working at KGSA, one of my classmates called asking for 200 shillings for food. In primary, she didn't have money for books or food. At KGSA, we were given some books. Life became easier. After graduation, life gets hard again. She decided to get married and stopped working. When a man comes with money, it's the thing to do. But she's not happy. All my friends are married for support. None are married for love. My friends are talented, but they are at home with kids, hungry. So I give them money to buy food."

While Teka partnered with KCDF to fund Violet's post-secondary schooling, Ryan decided to use some foundation money to support the graduates as well. "At the very beginning when KGSA started," Ryan said, "this was not about getting girls into university. It was about changing the mindset of a girl in Kibera and letting her know that she can do better. There's a place that values her. There's a community of support. Even the girls who don't get into college know that high school was not a waste of time. College is not the only measure of success. KGSA gives confidence and a space that values girls and tells them, 'You know what? You deserve it.'"

Linet saved enough money to apply to Baraton University. She got a call from them saying that she had been accepted. "I called my brother because I was so excited. Finally my dreams were coming true."

She went straight to Abdul with the news. He called Ryan in the United States and said, "Linet got accepted to Baraton. Can we send her?"

On Ryan's next trip to Kenya, Linet came by the school and walked up to him in the library with a slip of paper. It was her acceptance letter. She very quietly said to him, "This is all my paperwork. I was wondering if the foundation would be able to pay for my university fees." They decided that Linet and her brother could teach at KGSA during their university breaks as a work-study agreement. She loved the idea.

"When we go to university, we have a higher chance of success. Employers value degrees and will pay us more," Linet said. "I'm nervous, but excited about the knowledge I'm going to get. When I get that degree, I will be respected.

"The struggle was all worth it. My mother wanted me to be a teacher. Now my mother's dream is coming true. I got accepted to study education at university, and I felt my mother with me. She's happy. She sees me moving somewhere."

The KGSA budget had swelled to $50,750 despite the end of PADEM's $22,000-a-year commitment. It was the first year the KGSA Foundation was the major financial supporter, giving $25,000. Part of the KGSA Foundation's contribution came from Umbrella Tree, an organization willing to support the salary of a trained principal position. Ryan Sarafolean was awarded the Forward under Forty Award from the Wisconsin Alumni Association, helping to raise KGSA's American profile. Sporting Chance increased its giving to $8,750, while CARE and Stichting 4 Life maintained their donations from 2010 with $1,200 and $10,000 respectively. Alla Vida, a Kenyan project funding source, rounded out the budget with $5,800.

The funding from Alla Vida was a turning point for the school's finances. For one, it was a Kenyan organization, so it was a good step toward Abdul's vision of being less dependent on international money. Alla Vida sent staff members to the school who loved what KGSA was doing. Relationships were built between KGSA staff and Alla Vida staff. They started by covering budget line items like uniforms, food, and chemicals for the lab, but also asked Teka to see their KGSA's plan so they could understand what KGSA was spending money on, where they were headed, and how Alla Vida could help. Having a local hands-on and invested partner was very exciting to Teka and Abdul.

The money from Alla Vida had been a long time coming. Back in 2009, Comic Relief came to Kibera to shoot a documentary called *Famous, Rich and in the Slums*. Comic Relief is a U.K.-based organization that "drives positive change through the power of entertainment." Their Red Nose Campaign happens every two years, asking people to do something entertaining to raise money for people in poverty in the U.K. and Africa. As part of the campaign, they put four British stars—Lenny Henry, Samantha Womack, Reggie Yates, and Angela

Rippon—into the slum of Kibera to see how they would survive—and let the cameras roll. The Comic Relief crew behind the camera, friends with the *Slum Survivors* crew, got Abdul's name as a recommendation to be a guide for the stars. Abdul had never heard of Comic Relief or any of the stars, but he knew what the international attention could do for his school after shooting *Slum Survivors*, so he agreed to help. He got paid 120,000 shillings, U.S. $1,300, to help the crew make decisions and be the point man on the ground for the four celebrities.

Abdul took their belongings, phones, money, and credit cards, and sent Lenny, Samantha, Reggie, and Angela on their way. The first week, they were given a shelter, slum clothes, and 200 Kenyan shillings to live on their own, requiring them to earn their own money. The second week, they lived with Kiberans—Lenny with orphans, Samantha with a prostitute, Angela with an HIV-positive hairdresser, and Reggie with an aspiring hip hop artist. Abdul had no idea what he was getting himself into. The celebrities all broke down at some point, begging for their money back, better accommodations, and to be able to help the people in Kibera they had met. Abdul advocated for them, but the crew refused. It became clear to Abdul that they just wanted a good tape, and he hoped that the tape would eventually lead to some money for KGSA and the people of Kibera.

Lenny snapped the first night he was staying with the kids. Their place had a drainpipe with sewage running through it, and the rancid smell was overwhelming. Crying, Lenny said to Abdul, "This isn't fun anymore. This is real. Give me my credit cards. I can't stay here. They can't stay here. No one should live like this. I'm leaving with these kids."

"I wouldn't have wanted to stay there either," Abdul said. "It was really bad. But the producers made me keep him there. So I got some boys I knew from the neighborhood and paid them to come clean out the drainpipe so Lenny and the kids could sleep."

It was hard for Abdul to hear what the British celebrities said about Kibera. It was hard on him when the producers wouldn't let the stars take care of their hosts. "Why are they here, to laugh at us? To pity us? Showing just the extreme poverty is not showing all of Kibera. But if we don't get the information out, our poverty will remain a secret. It's frustrating. I wish the media would show the good side of Kibera too, but we do need help. Pity parties do work. They get people emotional; they give big money once and then walk away and forget about us. Pity works for a quick fix, but it doesn't work for long term relationships." Eventually, Samantha broke the crew down and demanded they let her support her host. In the end, all four stars aided their hosts in some way.

Famous, Rich and in the Slums aired on BBC One in March of 2011. Angela wrote to Abdul right away to tell him that the show raised a huge sum of money on the very first day. The entire Red Nose Campaign, of which the show was a significant contributing member, raised over ninety million pounds (U.S. $143,914,950, or several billion Kenyan shillings) total. "Make sure you see some of that money," Angela urged Abdul. "Don't let them keep it all."

Comic Relief works through local organizations. The agreement was that they would give one million pounds, or U.S. $1.5 million dollars, to the KCDF, and one million pounds to Alla Vida, which would, in turn, distribute it to support KGSA and other Kiberan organizations. Abdul never saw any of the money. When Sporting Chance flew him to the U.K. in 2011, he reached out to Lenny, Reggie, Angela, and Samantha. Reggie dodged his calls, but Angela made him go to the Comic Relief office, where they met Lenny. The face-to-face connection helped Comic Relief put pressure on KCDF and Alla Vida to support KGSA. Abdul was convinced that, without a trip to the U.K., he never would have gotten the promised support.

After four years as principal at KGSA, Teka knew it was time to make a change. Abdul explained, "We decided that Teka is the father figure to the girls, but they needed a mother figure too. We wanted a woman leading the school, so the girls could see an educated woman from Kibera with power. Teka is not a trained teacher, so we also wanted a professional teacher, but that is pretty expensive."

With funding from Umbrella Tree, Abdul and Teka conducted a short search. They found a woman named Christine Gakio teaching at St. Gabriel's and were confident that she would be a great fit. Christine herself had grown up in Kibera, so she had experienced the same struggles as the students. She was born in Kibera in 1962. She knew the Kibera that Abdul knew, the Kibera that had farms and land, animals and plenty of food. Christine had benefited from the devotion and protection of her single mother. Her mother sent Christine and all eleven of her siblings to school. She remembered, "My momma did a lot of farming. We had cows and goats so we had milk and meat. We had vegetables and bananas. She would buy some sugar, maybe some cooking oil, but she didn't have to buy much. She was industrious enough to take care of twelve of us."

With her mother keeping her on the right path, Christine went to boarding school in Kisumu for secondary school and the University of Nairobi after that. She and her children left her abusive husband. "Like my mother, I knew I could provide. She would say, 'I am your mother and your father.' She put us together. That was the kind of woman I had to hold me and nurture me and make me the independent woman I am today. She was illiterate, but she fought for the rights of a woman."

With Christine hired as principal, KGSA was considered a more official school. Christine knew how to train the teachers to create syllabi, and she could easily interpret the demands of the Ministry of Education.

Abdul and Teka sensed the impact of the change right away. "During the first week of school, one of the first-year students got her period for the first time. She was shocked," Abdul said. "Christine offered some motherly care. This first experience, I believe, is very important. The girl needs to understand what is happening in her body and what that means for her as a woman. To be given the right information in the right way will really help her over the years to make good judgments and sound decisions."

Christine was happy at KGSA. "St. Gabriel's was a good school, but I spent so much time dealing with the finances. I had to chase after school fees, and I myself was not always paid on time. Teka approached me about coming to KGSA, and I was happy to take the job. I love that KGSA is free because I don't want to run around collecting school fees. I don't know where the money comes from. I just work on making the school better. Abdul and Teka trust me.

"I show the teachers how to mark papers and plan lessons. We meet twice each month and discuss. Abdul asked me to donate part of my salary to lift up the teachers. I agreed. I am supposed to get 35,000 shillings a month, but I took 25,000. I have done much with my 25,000 shillings. It is peaceful. I receive the money on time. My teachers are not complaining because they are getting 9,000. They value their jobs and know what they are supposed to be doing.

"Now we need to get the girls to perform. They don't have enough time to study on their own. Take, for example, a fourth-year student whose father smokes a lot of marijuana. His friends come over, and the house is loud and there's no privacy. She's in charge of running the house, and when it doesn't go right, she gets a beating. Most of the girls leave the school at six, but she rushes home to start working at 4:30. It's like she's married to her father. We have class from eight until four. At four, they clean and go to clubs; then they go home and do chores. They don't have time to review what they learn in class. I tried to introduce preps and discussions on Saturdays and Sundays and want to add time for personal study in the morning and evening aside from class.

"The school is in a better place now that there are more women on faculty. With only male teachers around, who would talk about menstrual pads? The parents gain confidence. They think, 'The principal is a woman, she won't let the girls get molested by the men around.' I know the men here would never do that, but now we build trust in our reputation on the outside.

"Being born in Kibera and getting to the university, the students know the kind of family I come from, and they trust me to be their teacher." Christine turned her attention toward academic performance in the classroom while Teka looked beyond.

Teka said, "We cannot talk about performance without looking at their whole lives. We have to address so much more than academics." KGSA started a mentorship program in 2011 in hopes of improving academic performance. Ten volunteers came every Saturday to offer life-skills training and provide a space for the girls to tell their stories. Claris continued the life-skills curriculum during the school week. After seeing his KGSA students open up and cry with their mentors, Teka hoped to eventually create a one-on-one program.

During one life-skills session, the third-year girls formed two lines out in the sunny courtyard. They began a fiercely competitive relay race balancing a twenty-ounce soda bottle filled with water on their heads. The girls waiting in line screamed encouragement and tips to their teammate. It was silly, and the girls laughed, but they also really wanted to win. They looked forward to life-skills classes because they could get up from their desks and play.

Afterward, two girls identified as leaders for the day led a discussion about what was required of them during the race: concentration, balance, perseverance, teamwork, and responsibility. The curriculum then tied these ideas to sexuality. They discussed myths about sex, spoke truths to combat the myths, and agreed that it takes life skills to stay healthy and remain in school.

"What are some myths about sex?"

"You won't get pregnant your first time."

"You can't get AIDS from your husband."

"If you pee after sex, you won't get pregnant."

"Being on the pill helps stop you from getting AIDS."

In addition to being trained to take turns leading the class with their peers, the KGSA girls get trained to go to primary schools and do age-appropriate lessons with the students. Claris liked the program because the activities, like the bottle races, used sports, broke up the day in the classroom, didn't take up much space, and didn't require equipment beyond what was easily accessible. In that way, it was a program made for Kibera. Trained counselors came to KGSA quarterly as part of the program, and all the lessons included some aspect of sexuality to address sexually transmitted diseases and pregnancy. Also quarterly, the girls went to a *Jitambue* rally held for girls in Kibera to help them claim their identities. The daylong rally had music, speakers, free lunch, and menstrual pad distribution. Claris said, "This is all as important as what happens in the classroom. The parents of most of these girls didn't get the opportunity to go to school. So they are not well equipped with information about birth control and sex education. We need to educate the whole girl so that she can stay in school and learn."

Teka believed these classes were so important that they were built into the weekly schedule. He said, "We have to address their attitude and self-esteem, and we have to address the pressure they are under to have sex. We teach the girls that abstinence is the best way, but there is so much pressure on them to have sex. We must talk about condoms too. We don't encourage birth control pills because the girls are always worried about getting pregnant when they have sex. But they also should be worried about HIV and infections. Birth control does not help with that. The mothers tell the girls to take the pills. It's only forty shillings (forty-seven cents) [a month] for the pill, and some organizations give it out for free. That is what the chemist sells the most of. They don't think about HIV. I don't know why. They just get scared about pregnancy. In Kibera, having sex is normal for girls. It's so hard to teach them to abstain. We try."

It seemed to be working. The number of girls getting pregnant at KGSA had dropped drastically since 2006.

The next step of the mentorship program was to bring in tutors from Starehe Girls' National School. Starehe kept girls for a fifth and sixth year before sending them to college to make sure that they had the technical skills necessary to excel in university. These girls got straight As, their KCSE scores were high, and students there had the academic confidence that KGSA girls lacked. The Starehe fifth- and sixth-year students came to tutor the KGSA fourth-year students to better prepare them for the KCSE.

Most of the girls who entered KGSA had poor skills in math and science. They didn't receive the training they needed in primary school, and they bought into the societal stigma that girls can't do math and science. By secondary school, they were convinced they simply couldn't do it and would never be able to. The Starehe girls were getting As in math, chemistry, and physics, so the KGSA students had to explore their own disempowerment. Teka was hopeful. "Me, I cannot convince my girls that there is no difference, but the Starehe girls do. People are changing their attitudes, especially in math." Changing the stigma around math and science at KGSA was essential. One low subject score could affect the composite KCSE score, and failing math or science could keep a graduate from being accepted into college even if her other scores were high. If she wanted to study Swahili in college, they took her math and science scores very seriously. The mentors and tutors were helping with skills, but also attitudes as well.

KGSA sent the third group of fourth-year students to take the KCSE. To beat test anxiety, the girls created "prayer day" when parents, teachers, and students gather to pray in preparation for the exams.

Teka put the girls into committees and gave them a budget to work with. The girls in charge of food bought chicken, rice, and tea, and formed subcommittees to prepare the food. They got to school early in the morning to cook. Teka showed up with music on his laptop and speakers.

"Teka, put the music up loud!"

The girls congregated in the library together and started dancing until the floor was shaking. They danced until the parents started arriving. Remembering it was called prayer day, they turned the music down and, as Lynn said, "became good students."

The parents and girls feasted together. Teka led Christian prayers and Abdul led Muslim ones. The mood was a mixture of both solemn and excited feelings. The KCSE caused nerves, but it also acted as a turning point. Most of these girls never imagined finishing secondary school. As soon as the last parent left the school, the music started up again.

According to Lynn, "The whole building started shaking again.

Oh, we danced. We didn't want to be told to clean up. Teka eventually left with the music, but we knew it by heart. We sang and danced without it. We prayed so the test went well, but basically it was a dance party. No function can go without music at Girls Soccer."

Dancing was a good distraction from the pressure.

"People thought I would be like my mother and stop school in the eighth grade and have kids when I started menstruating," Asha said. "I wanted to prove them wrong."

Even in secondary school, Asha's mother kept telling her, "You are going to fail. All that education is not going to help you."

"I never wanted to be famous or rich. I just wanted to be educated. Teachers told us as first years that these four years would make or destroy the next sixty years of our life. Working hard for the test was our only task. Our teachers, even our parents, told us, 'You have to perform.' So it is like a mantra in our heads for four years, 'Perform, perform, perform.' We started to believe that life would not stop after graduation. We had to work hard and get to college."

She knew education was the key to a life outside of Kibera. "That is the only armor we have in the battlefield. If I don't have a degree, people won't take me seriously."

She was top in her class, but that would not help her get into college. "We all need scholarships, which mean a B on the KCSE. It is that or start a family."

During her final year, Asha skipped chores at home. She stayed at school longer and longer studying because she and her mother would quarrel. Frustrated with her own life, her mother just called it as she saw it: a waste of time.

Principal Christine tried to keep her focused. "I'm expecting big things from you, Asha."

"Wait, you'll see."

She, as Ida had been the year before, was calm heading into the end of her fourth year. She told her classmates to have hope. She was the top girl. She knew she was ready. She prayed so much, she remembered it as a time when she felt holy.

Then two months before the exam, Asha got typhoid.

"I felt like my stomach was eating my stomach, like someone was eating my intestines. I felt like my body was haunted. They gave me all kinds of very expensive medicine. My father had to reach deep into his pocket. And when I came to school, people were worried."

She knew she needed to study, but she also needed to rest. It was hard to find the balance. She became very thin again.

"I didn't feel good. But I had to keep going. I had to pass. I used to come to school at five or six in the morning and stay until eight at night. I would close myself in and read. If I grew tired of reading, I wrote. The school was my home Monday through Sunday. Abdul would say, 'Get out of the school, go home. Walking at night is not safe. One day books will kill you. Just take a break.'"

When Asha got home, her mother accused her of running around with men. "I was not with a man. I was with my books," is all she would say.

Her mother said, "Those books will never help you. Just go to the kitchen and cook. Every woman needs to know how to cook. You can do the chores at home."

Eventually she was studying so much, she asked Kazee, the security man, for keys to the school. She said, "Kazee, you know me. I won't play." He agreed.

"When you go home, make sure you lock the whole school." The day before the KCSE, she handed the keys back. He said, "I wish you luck."

Asha felt that the test went well, that she had performed well. She was left to wait for results.

Lynn had conflicting feelings going into her KCSE exam. "The test meant that I was done with high school, stress, homework, and early mornings. But there was also pressure. If I failed, I would have a miserable life. If I passed, I would have a sweet life. My father was always in my throat. 'You see how we are struggling. And if you don't work hard in this exam, we will continue living this miserable life.'"

Lynn was frisked on her way into the test. She took her seat at desk number five and listened to the extensive list of rules that, if broken, could lead to her exam being terminated.

The first paper was English, which she loved. "You know you can do it. You are the best," she told herself. She wrote her name and student number. She opened the booklet to the comprehension section on the first page. She remembered the material from her first year. She settled in for a month of testing.

After two days of English, the third day tested math in the morning and geography in the afternoon. During the second math section, she said her mind went blank. "Horrible," she shook her head, "so stressful." This was not her strongest subject, and she left that day with a fierce headache.

On the day the KCSE scores were released, there was a weak Internet connection at KGSA so the girls couldn't check their scores at school. Asha texted her admission number to her aunt, who checked the website and texted back her score.

It was C−. She couldn't believe it. She cried all night. She cried so hard her sister called her father and begged him to come home and comfort her.

"I know my capabilities! This is not representative!" she yelled at him.

"Don't let one test score be the judge of your life," he offered.

"Get out of my room! I don't want to see you. I thought I would do better than this. I thought that test would get me out of Kibera."

She called Lynn, "I can't believe this. I hate God. I will never go to the mosque again."

Lynn got a C. She was also disappointed to not qualify for scholarship, but she thought that maybe, like Violet, she could find financial support to go to college. She couldn't apply to a four-year university program, but she immediately started looking into a two-year program at Zetech College where she could study photography and journalism.

Asha, however, was inconsolable. "Not everybody who gets a B is smart. And not everybody who gets a D is dumb. We spend four years working on an exam that will take a month. The pressure is too much. Life without education is not life. Life without that B is not life. We are taught to dream so big, and the school helps us be hopeful that our dreams come true. We spent 365 days praying. When I didn't perform, I felt like the finish line had been drawn. It's done. If I cannot perform well, I am dumb. My life is over at eighteen. I will never work. I will never go to college. Start a family. It's time."

Asha's aunt and Principal Christine asked Asha to consider repeating, as Linet did. But her dashed hopes got the better of her. The night she got her results back, she considered climbing a tree in her backyard and jumping off. It was her siblings that changed her mind.

"If I kill myself, who will take care of my siblings? I want them to live a life that I never lived. I can't stand seeing my brother staying out of school because of money. I want to take my sister to college too. I have hands. I can work. I can fight for them."

She felt like her mother's prophecy was coming true. Asha started cooking, washing, and cleaning again. She started behaving like a girl looking to get married. She started bonding with her mother and asked to learn how to braid hair.

"I told you so. I told you those books would never help you."

Asha agreed, "It is true. I wish I had never wasted my time going to school and getting an education. I wish those four years I could have stayed with you and learned how to braid hair and cook."

"I think we can inherit madness," Asha admitted in secret. "Sometimes I think I am going to be mad one day like my mother."

Asha graduated from KGSA with a C+ average. But what matters is the KCSE. Asha's C– on the KCSE qualified her for a diploma program. Doing well in her two years of diploma work would mean that she could then apply to get a four-year degree. So doing better on the KCSE would have saved her time and money. Asha failed math on her KCSE, which brought her composite score down significantly. It also inhibited her from applying to law programs as she had dreamed of. Math is what kept her from going to university.

Twenty-two of the twenty-eight test takers passed with a D or higher, and nine of the twenty-eight got the C– necessary to apply for programs. None of the 2011 graduates got the B necessary for post-secondary government funding. Ryan and the KGSA Foundation decided to offer funding to any KGSA graduate who got a C– or above on the KCSE if they found, applied, and got into a post-secondary program. Ryan encouraged Asha, despite her disappointment in her C–, to look into diploma programs and keep studying. She did. Asha was accepted into a two-year program at Moi University.

Teka said, "I care about the girls so much. I push them to pass exams. I tell them to work through their problems at home like I did. I just knew my only hope was education. I feel bad when they don't perform well. My real happiness will come when all the students pass exams and have a good life after KGSA. That is what I want."

Abdul had become a high-profile community organizer in Kibera. All this work was in addition to his job at Telkom. Climbing telephone poles was not as much fun at age forty, and so when Linda suggested he consider working for Stichting 4 Life, he jumped at the idea.

Stichting 4 Life, in addition to covering the food budget at KGSA, hired single mothers who were HIV-positive to bead jewelry and sold the jewelry in Dutch markets, with profits going to salaries and medical care for the women. When there was a big order to fill, they often hired KGSA girls who were especially vulnerable. They hired Linet, for example, while she was waiting to start college. John and Linda needed someone on the ground in Kenya they could trust. Their board wanted a woman, but John and Linda pushed to get Abdul hired. It worked.

He quit his job at Telkom and became the Kenyan director of Stichting 4 Life. John and Linda flew Abdul to the Netherlands so he could fully understand the clientele for the jewelry. He liked it there, but said it was a little too perfect. "The lawns were trimmed just so. The wait staffs at the restaurants were so cordial. It was a little creepy to me. I like things a bit messier. Now I understand why John and Linda get so much peace by coming to Kibera."

Zakiya, Abdul's wife, was thrilled at the job change. She was tired of never seeing her husband. Between Telkom and KGSA, he rarely came home. He dashed from work to go check on the students. Free time was spent coordinating film crews, setting up interviews, writing grants, and talking to potential clients. She didn't ask for much, just to have tea with him now and again. She was lonely and had started to become a little jealous of the students.

Over the years, Zakiya had become close with some of the students herself. She loved to cook with the girls and talk about school and boys. They prayed together, and she gave them advice. She became a mother figure to many of them. Lynn and Salma called her "Mom."

"He gives more time to the girls at KGSA than to me. I asked him to go on vacation with me so that I could have him all to myself for once. He has gotten to see the Netherlands and England. I would like to see the world too. I'd love to go to Tanzania. We haven't yet gone."

When Abdul started working for John and Linda, he had more time to be with Zakiya. He started to spend time with her daily. He told her that God will bless them for the work he was doing with the children in Kibera. He promised that when they had a child of their own, he would be around more.

Abdul found some funding sources for the feeding program and teachers' salaries. The KGSA Foundation supported the school. Teka and Christine ran the day-to-day operations. Abdul could take a step back and breathe. He walked around Kibera. He listened to the girls. The school was stable. Abdul believed that the best way he could support Teka and Christine as they worked for better academic performance was to support primary schools that fed into KGSA. He just needed more time.

John, Linda, and Abdul wanted to identify a few primary schools they could support financially. In the long term, that could support KGSA by giving them stronger students.

Abdul walked down the tracks to a primary school not far from KGSA. There were four classes in a single room divided by thin pieces of plywood. The little children were all in matching but tattered uniforms. The children stood when he walked in and sang him a welcome song in unison. They looked at him with big eyes and smiles as they sang, some pointing and giggling. Abdul greeted the teachers and addressed the children briefly, and then assessed the location.

"When the train derails, which happens now and then, the kids in the school are in danger." The government had come through and marked the buildings that were too close to the tracks. They could come at any point and take down all the marked structures. The Kiberans, with no land titles, have no recourse. The school had a blue marking on the tin wall. Stichting 4 Life was partnering with this primary school to help them move to a larger space that would be less dangerous and more conducive to learning.

A few weeks later, Abdul and Claris walked down the railway tracks to another school, stopping now and again when people wanted to talk to them. They passed the former location of the primary school. The government had come in and bulldozed it in order to build a high rise. The school put up a makeshift structure while working out a contingency plan. Two of the grade-school classes met outside, crammed on benches that sloped uphill. Three classes met inside, with no partition of any sort. When it rained, the two outdoor classes ran inside and tried to find a place on the floor to sit and learn. There were no books or pens. Each class had a tiny chalkboard hanging by string.

"This can't be. These kids can't learn like this," Abdul said while observing from the corner. Kenya made free primary school mandatory in 2006. Unfortunately, the mandate in no way assured that the education would be a good one or schools would have the funding they needed. What money there was went to very large schools, with hundreds of students, but children in Kibera did not have money for transportation to get to those schools. Therefore, the slum had many small schools in small structures with no financial support from the government. Children in Kibera benefited from going to a local school with invested teachers who understood the difficulties they faced. Since Kibera was not recognized by the government, however, the schools needed to find their own funding. Abdul brought a calm focus to the issue of long-term, sustainable development.

In education, location matters. There are primary-school children learning in spaces that are loud, crowded, and dangerous. Learning is happening, but more learning can happen if all the spaces these young people inhabit—home and school—are safe and supportive.

THE SONG SHE SANG TO ME
2012

I am married to my books. I am pregnant with knowledge.

—ASHA JAFFAR

Over the years, Abdul had seen many organizations, promising big money and fast change, come and go.

"I am happy with our gradual growth. Fast doesn't work in Kibera. To make change that is real, we have to be at peace with moving slowly. If I light up a piece of paper, it lights up fast, and then it's gone. If I light up charcoal, it takes a while to get warm. But it also takes a long while to burn down. That is what KGSA has been, a slow burn. It was dark, but now we are burning. Next we are going to build the boarding facility."

KGSA already felt like a home. The teachers and the students spent as much time as possible there. On Sunday, the only day without class, there was programming. The girls came for a break from their one-room homes, for electricity, and for time to play with their friends. In their classmates, they had found other girls who believed that girls matter, that education was a worthy struggle, and that KGSA was a safe place to dream. Some of these girls were orphans or displaced from their upcountry families. Others were abused and tired. At KGSA, they could join the revolution that was happening. They were a family, guaranteed. Next, they needed a safe place to study and sleep. Abdul's goal was to increase the quality of education. "A lot of the schools that are doing well are boarding schools. We need to keep getting better, sending more girls to university. Then we will have achieved. If we can take them through university, that will be the whole cycle. From there, we will figure out where we go.

"If I go to the girls with the problem, they will give me twenty different good ideas that will work. They think in a different way and are living the problems. I have to level with them, and I learn so much from that."

Asha was influential in the movement toward having a dormitory. As a second-year student, when she started finding her voice in response to corporal punishment, she also told Abdul plainly, "We want a dorm."

He took a deep breath and said, "I can't promise you anything. Right now we need a lab and a library."

When she was a third-year student, Abdul came by the library after work. The girls were there late studying. He said, "I can see you are benefiting from the electricity in the school."

"Yes, but we need a dorm."

"You girls are going to kill me one day. A dorm!"

"Yes Abdul, we need a dorm. Abdul, for now, just rent rooms for girls who need boarding badly and can't stand staying at home."

Abdul started calling Asha his lawyer because she would start pleas with statements like "Abdul, I will give you substantial evidence" or "Please don't overrule it, please." When Asha reached her final year, Abdul told her she had spoken well. He directed Asha, Salma, and Lynn to draft a formal proposal for a dormitory.

"I didn't know that while we were pushing, he was talking to Ryan," Asha said. "When I told him that teachers were beating us, that students needed tea during break, that we needed supper, I knew he listened. So I knew he listened to me about the dorm too.

"I was watching CNN at school and there was this person, Larry King, who said if you want to nominate a CNN hero, go online. We didn't have computers, but I had Abdul in mind because he is a hero in Kibera. He serves us. The school started six years ago and at least four hundred girls in Kibera have benefited. We have gotten the education, and we have gotten to be strong in life. If I had had a computer, I would've taken the video of the school and sent it to CNN. When I saw the person who won, I said, 'Abdul could have beaten that person.' He gave his land, and he even went into his pocket and used his own money. I remember times when we didn't have money for lunch. He would feed us. If he had money, he would help. He is a good person. He listened to me as a sixteen year old. That means everything to me.

"People like Nelson Mandela fought for freedom that millions of people are living in now. Malcolm X, Martin Luther King Jr., they fought for the freedom of people even though they didn't get to live in that freedom. That's how I felt about the dormitory. I knew I wouldn't get to live there, but I wanted to make it possible for students after me."

Two big things happened in 2012 that made the dormitory an achievable dream. One was that Sean Rush asked Abdul what more he could do to help. Early on, Sean paid for cameras and computers for the Journalism Club. Then he made a $10,000 donation when the school was in the red, twice. "He believes in the school," Ryan said. "But he says that in all of his travels, he has never met a man like Abdul. Sean meets a lot of people. Abdul stuck out. He trusts Abdul to spend the money appropriately."

Sean added, "I've seen so much as head of JA Worldwide. Part of my work is to make a dent. I can't fix the world, but on a personal level, I can make a difference in the lives of 130 girls. When I spoke to Rhodes Scholars at Oxford, I titled my talk '130 Girls and How They Changed My Life.' I told them about KGSA and urged them to find something to add meaning to their own lives."

Sean visited KGSA in 2012 to shoot a short video for the JA World Wide Web site. As soon as he walked into the courtyard, he heard a familiar voice shout, "Sean Rush!" Asha came running. On that trip, Abdul was talking a lot about the dream of the dormitory. He walked Sean next door to show him the plot of land they wanted to buy.

Standing on the balcony a bit later, looking out over Kibera, Sean asked Abdul, "How much does it cost?"

"Twelve thousand dollars," Abdul replied.

"I think my wife and I could cover that. Count on me."

And just like that, the land was purchased.

Meanwhile, Ryan approached a friend of his to see if he would be interested in doing an initial design of the dormitory pro bono. Mookie Tierney had gone to the same high school as Ryan, two years Ryan's junior. Mookie was heading to Kenya to build an aquaponics fish farm on Mfangano Island with Organic Health Response (OHR). Ryan asked him to come to KGSA and design the dormitory as well. Mookie said yes. "I was excited to work with Abdul because he understands that building work needs to be done by local people with their own ingenuity and sweat."

The first dormitory meeting was a vision session. Abdul had invited Teka, Christine, Claris, Lynn, and Asha to be there as staff. Each grade had nominated one student to represent their class's needs and desires: Habiba, Lillian, Mary, and Dalifa. Two Journalism Club students circled the table taking video and still shots. This meeting was big news.

"What do you want in your dormitory?" Mookie asked the KGSA students at the meeting.

"Bunk beds."

"Room to study."

"Yeah, that sounds good."

"No, dream bigger," Mookie urged. "You can have anything. What do you want in your dorm?"

"A courtyard with grass."

"And chairs there to sit on and relax."

"Indoor games like pool."

"Or table tennis!"

"How about a store where we can buy sweets at night?"

They all giggled in amazement. Without realizing it, some of them were on their feet. This was too good to be true.

After all the students had spoken, the adults added logistical concerns. "No windows on the street side of the first floor."

"And the girls shouldn't sleep on the ground floor either."

"Is there a way to use rain water? Can we have gutters and rain tanks?"

"I heard you can use methane from toilets for cooking. Is that true?"

"Storage. We're going to need very secure storage so our supplies don't get stolen."

"Can we move the bathrooms closer to the bedrooms?"

"Can we use solar panels?"

Mookie listened, asked questions, and took copious notes. He met with the committee of KGSA students and faculty over several days. He was only twenty-five, but everyone at the table hung on his every word. He took all the information and did some sketches, taking into account ventilation and sunlight. "Because they're used to tin, when people get money, they build cubes out of cement. That means no airflow and no use of the sun.

"Being educated is such a privilege, and sustainable architecture is something that needs to be spread. I have sustainable architecture knowledge, and they have knowledge about where they are living and what they need. Everyone is equally important. I'm not smarter than the people I work with; I just have access to information that they don't yet. So I share what I know. But I don't live here, so they share their knowledge with me. It works."

In the meetings, Abdul kept saying to the girls, "Speak up, I can't hear you. Talk like you mean it." And they did. They wanted a prayer room close to the bedrooms. They talked about the needs of Christians and Muslims living in the same dormitory. The girls pictured sleeping two girls per bed in bunk beds. That is what they assumed they would have to do.

Mookie started sketching each floor of the dormitory on the board, rooms surrounding an open courtyard where girls could sit and clothes could be hung to dry. The girls watched in awe. They stole glances at each other and laughed. They were going to have their boarding school.

"So let's talk specifics. What do you want a cube to look like? How many bunk beds are in each one? Do you want storage underneath for your stuff?"

At a lull in the conversation, Abdul leaned back on his stool. "Wow. This is big. Just get us the money, Ryan."

"I promise," Ryan said with conviction.

Abdul turned to the adults and made eye contact with each one in turn. "The theme of this year is quality of education. If I give you this facility, there are no more excuses. You have to deliver. The improvement has to be measurable. We have to get more of these girls into college."

Teka, Christine, and Claris nodded silently.

As Mookie drew a cross-section of the three levels, Claris stood up and pointed at the board. "I see it now. Oh my. This is beautiful."

It's easy to get excited, but Teka had learned to be patient and pessimistic.

"The dormitory is a dream come true. But I won't believe it until I see it. I'm still affected by people breaking promises," he said. "But I understand why they do. They don't do it on purpose. Suppose I see in a photograph people who have no food. If I go to that place, I will feel for the children, for the mothers. When I come back to Nairobi, I will forget about them. I think it's normal.

"Kibera is a challenge. Every year, we have about ten girls move back to their upcountry homes. When they go upcountry, we lose them. A few of them are now married. We have four students we pay rent for. I don't know how to budget that. I would like the students to go on to be lawyers, artists, successful women. I would like for KGSA girls to be at the top of every profession. One day, maybe, they could come back and talk to students as professionals. That is my dream: Look, they made it from Kibera."

Claris, in addition to teaching and taking night classes, became a mother. She gave birth to a baby boy who was welcomed into the KGSA family right away. She couldn't tell her birth story without mentioning some of the real challenges women in Kibera face around issues of maternal health and well-being.

"Most of the good hospitals are far away and most of the women don't have enough money to pay for them. We prefer going to midwives. Midwives charge a very low price, and they have natural herbs that we trust from our traditions. When I was pregnant, I would pay my midwife 100 shillings, just over one U.S. dollar, a visit. She massaged my stomach and turned the baby if need be. Then when it comes time to deliver the baby, women pay 1,500 shillings, seventeen U.S. dollars, to the midwife. The midwife applies some herbal medicine around the vagina. And the woman delivers on the floor of her house. She gathers what comes after. In most cases, she usually buries it underground or puts it in the toilet. I did not go to the midwife to deliver. I was very scared. I went to a hospital.

"Women who go to the Kibera Clinic usually deliver by themselves, then the doctor comes and cuts the umbilical cord for them. I had hard labor for more than a day. I don't think the doctors were experts because they asked me to keep pushing, but the baby was not ready. So when it came time to push, I was very tired and I didn't have energy. One of the doctors pressed on my stomach, and the baby came out. On the spot, I fainted. My sister washed me and carried me to bed where my child was. That whole day I was unconscious.

"When I woke up, I tried to visit the loo. I was given warm water to bathe with. Then I was told that I needed to wash all of my bloodstains on the bed sheet. The patient is in charge of cleaning up after herself. I had lost a lot of blood, and they didn't have blood for me so I was given a bowl of beans and was told to eat it to get energy.

"Miscarriages are common in Kibera. When women miscarry, the child is put in a box, and then it is upon the women to find where to take that body. Some women will put it in a drain; others dig by their doors. According to the African community, the first child should be buried in the homes in the rural areas. Many don't have money to transfer the body.

"Abortions are looked down upon, but at times, the parents will support it. Or if a young girl is having sex with an old man, then the man may also give her some money to do away with the child. Some hospitals do abortions for a fee of 3,000 shillings, thirty-five U.S. dollars. There is one clinic that gives free abortions to prostitutes, but it is not safe.

"Some of the challenges that the girls face, most of the single women face too. Men assume that single mothers are in need. Someone has to provide for the child. The moment they see me passing by, as smart as they can, they will try to lure me. I am lucky that I have been equipped with some information, and I know that a man is after something. I keep myself busy and walk away. I am either at the house or at KGSA with the girls.

"Young men come to my house uninvited. I had one who asked for supper. I prepared him some porridge. He realized I was not after what he wanted, so he walked away. It's tiring. I'm very happy I decided to bring up my son as a single mother. But I have to work. I had to leave my son at a very early age. Since I am in a position to bring up my child in an organized manner, the men have stopped harassing me as much and have started to show me a little bit of respect.

"I used to provide all the meals for my family because my mother's business was not flourishing. I had to provide school fees for my brothers and sisters and the grandchildren. I would sleep on the problems and wake up with the problems. What am I supposed to do? How am I supposed to provide? Someone would wake me up early in the morning and ask to buy this or do that. I grew very thin. My mother noticed and told me it was better to support my family from a distance. I moved to Gatwekera village, where I pay 500 shillings, six U.S.

dollars, per month. Then with the remaining amount, I can support my siblings for school fees and buy meals for my mother.

"I want to move my son from the slum to a better place, away from air pollution to a better environment. We do not have a ground for playing. The kids develop abusive language, and I hear them abusing each other. What I want for my son is the best."

By 2012, Claris had been teaching at KGSA for five years. "We used to have no teachers trained in education, but now we have two. We used to have Teka as a principal, but now our principal is a female university graduate. We used to have fewer than 100 girls. Now we can accommodate 130. It has been so fun to watch the school grow and to grow with it."

For the first time, KGSA had thirty girls or more in each of the four classes. Twenty-seven of the thirty graduates passed the KCSE exam, and ten earned a C− or higher. It was the most successful year for the Journalism Club. Nelly and Commando joined the Under Twenty Kenyan National Soccer Team. It was also a big year for Abdul's visibility outside of Kibera.

TED (Technology, Entertainment, and Design), the popular talk series focused on "ideas worth spreading," hosted a talent search event in Nairobi, Kenya, in 2012. One speaker from the event would go on to a bigger TED stage to represent Nairobi. Ryan knew this could be a great opportunity, but Abdul was reluctant. Already too busy and spread too thin, Abdul blew it off. Ryan pushed, and Abdul pushed back. "Who is this Ted guy anyway?" he kept asking.

Desperate, Ryan decided to fly to London, where Abdul was meeting with Sporting Chance and Comic Relief, to help him with his one-minute application video. In a hotel room, Ryan kept pushing Abdul for more. He knew that Abdul's charisma and the story of KGSA were ripe for the TED stage. Abdul continued to be lethargic and reluctant.

"I couldn't understand why Ryan was making such a big deal out of this Ted guy," Abdul laughed.

Abdul's pitch was accepted, and only then did he go to TED's website and view the talks. "Then I understood who Ted was. I started researching my presentation. I decided to talk about the need for dialogue in development. I took pictures in Kibera of projects that failed because the people with money didn't listen to the people who needed help. When news of flying toilets [when people defecate into bags and throw them on the ground] spread in 1998, for example, a lot of funding came into Kibera for toilets. There's a biogas toilet that has a lamp [a toilet that uses energy from waste to create power to light the latrine], but who needs light in the toilet when we don't have electricity at home? There's a flushable toilet, but who needs that when we don't have clean water to drink? Our partners listen to what we need, which is why we're growing."

Abdul went to his first TED rehearsal feeling very nervous. The staff listened to his talk and helped him tweak it. His six-minute talk was titled "Real Change Requires Listening."

On the day of the TED presentations, Abdul said he was so nervous, he couldn't hear himself talking onstage. He said things like "Honestly, who will cook in a toilet?" and "The girls have a say; they sit down with our partners and iron out the challenges that they face" and "The missing link is dialogue; we need to start putting faces on the data and names on the faces, and that way, I think we would have a better world."

He received a standing ovation. People from Google and TED approached him, interested in networking. These organizations are used to working with large grants connecting big money with big initiatives. Abdul tried to explain that there couldn't be large schools in Kibera. Small schools needed to be supported too. Grants needed to be dispersed strategically.

"There are so many donations, but the poverty level is not decreasing, because people don't want to dialogue. They just want to throw money at each other. We need to do better."

Abdul ultimately wasn't chosen to move on to the next TED stage. However, he was hopeful that the connections he had made in the audience could add to the financial momentum of the school.

The $91,000 budget in 2012 had several significant stories embedded in it. It was the first KGSA budget drawn up ahead of time instead of using money as it came in. It almost doubled from the previous year's budget. The KGSA Foundation, passing the $100,000 lifetime fundraising mark itself, more than doubled its 2011 contribution to $52,000. And $23,100 came in from Comic Relief via KCDF and Alla Vida. Having more of their budget coming from Kenyan foundations was a clear step in the right direction.

KGSA made some exciting changes with their increased budget. First, they raised the base salary for their twenty-one staff people from 7,000 shillings a month to 9,000 shillings, about U.S. $100. Second, in addition to offering scholarships to KGSA graduates, they started paying for KGSA teachers to go to college. In 2012, five KGSA staffers were taking classes on nights and weekends. They also opened a journalism studio a short walk from the school. It was a quiet and safe place for the girls to edit their photos and videos. Graduates like Asha, Lynn, and Irene were also welcome there during the day to use the equipment for their own post-secondary studies in Web design, communications, and journalism.

Teka explained, "After high school, most of the girls don't go to college. They can't find work, they get stuck, and their families pressure them to marry. The Journalism Club girls get hands-on training with the cameras and video shooting and editing. How could they make use of those skills?

"I wrote a proposal to KCDF to help us start a photography business. The money is used to expand the Journalism Club, give internships to graduates, and help graduates find jobs in the industry. We teach them how to run a business and let them run it. Our company shoots video and pictures of local weddings. Schools hire us to capture big events like graduations. With the profits, we pay the girls and then sponsor as many as possible to go to college. We are also starting a savings group among the graduates to help them start small businesses. It is a bridge from high school to the next level of life."

★ ★ ★

One night, after the rooms were clean, the clubs had wrapped up, and the girls had gone home, Teka and teachers Amos, Godwin, and Musa were laughing over a Scrabble board. This was their Friday night. Teka had a keen eye for what he called "lifers." After years of seeing teachers come and go, Teka knew that these men, along with Claris, were lifers. They were not at KGSA for the salary; they were there for the students, the lifestyle, and the chances for personal growth that the school encouraged. They found a sense of family there. As KGSA grew, Teka was carefully looking out for the lifers, offering them transformations too.

Teka wanted to send them to school. He explained, "One day, KGSA will grow and be an institution that can afford to pay teachers. If we do hire new professional teachers, we can't forget about the ones who stuck with us and taught for free, year after year, making sure the school stayed open. I support training the current teachers so they become professional—so by the time we grow, we can afford to pay them what they deserve. They are doing great work."

In 2012, that dream came true.

Amos was tall and thin, with a young face and ears that stuck out. When he thought, he furrowed his brow. He was jovial, as they say in Kenya, and gentle. When he talked about his family, he rubbed his eyes with the back of his hand, knowing that few Kenyan men cry in public. Amos was Teka's right-hand man. They both loved CIA and FBI shows from the United States, and they purchased jackets that they thought made them look big and tough when they went out on "missions" to do "intelligence" work to keep the KGSA girls safe.

Amos went to what he referred to as a "bush school." By the time he was in his third year, he and his three best friends had formed a group called 4Pac, after the famous 2Pac (Tupac Shakur). The group was committed to changing the reputation of the school. They loved their studies and stayed over holiday breaks to read instead of going home.

Amos credited his work ethic in school to his grandmother. She never went to school herself, but she valued education. None of her own children made it to university, but when Amos showed potential in primary school, she told him repeatedly, "You have to go to college."

"That is the song she sang to me," he said.

It worked. The four boys in 4Pac graduated, and all scored very well on their KCSE exams. "It turned the picture of the school around," Amos said proudly. "I scored a B with sixty-two points. They were giving scholarships to Bs with sixty-five points. So I missed by three points."

Amos's principal decided to support him. He planned a trip for the two of them to Nairobi to look at schools. When Amos found the right program, his principal said he'd be willing to pay Amos's tuition. Amos was excited and ready to go.

"Then, robbers broke into his house, and they killed him. So I could not go to school. It tormented me. I thought about going back to fourth year and scoring enough to take me to university. But my brother was clearing eighth grade. My sister was married, so I was his only hope. I thought, 'Let me help my brother, then I will go back.'"

Amos moved to Nairobi with 1,000 shillings from his sister in his pocket. He bought a table and biscuits and sweets to sell, and went to town. His small business made him enough money to support his brother's secondary school tuition. Eventually, a friend told him that a school called KGSA was looking for a math and physics teacher. He went and found Teka in the office.

"May I speak with the principal?" he asked.

Teka said, "What do you want?"

"I am a teacher. I came with my papers."

And Teka hired Amos on the spot.

In 2009, when the teachers were earning 7,000 shillings a month at KGSA, Amos approached Teka again. He was having trouble paying his brother's tuition. His brother's school had called and said that if Amos taught there, his brother could learn for free, and Amos would also get paid 20,000 shillings a month. He had to accept, and Teka understood. He understood so much, in fact, that he was astounded when Amos returned to see if he could get his job back. After his brother graduated, Amos wanted to teach at KGSA for the 7,000 shillings instead of 20,000.

Amos had found it hard to teach in a school that required tuition, because he spent much of his time chasing down the money. Kids would be in class one day and gone the next because of lack of tuition. It was hard to build curriculum and momentum with such a transient group of learners. He also liked the innovations at KGSA. Teka happily welcomed him back. Amos wanted to start teaching agriculture for the girls who wanted to return upcountry after graduation.

"I can try something new, and they will listen to me."

As much as Amos enjoyed teaching the girls at KGSA, he also wondered about his future. He had made a promise to himself to go back to school. With each year that went by, it seemed less likely. "At the end of the day, where am I heading? I am not certified, I can never ask for more money."

The KGSA Foundation told Amos in 2012 that they would be sending him to college to get trained as a teacher. He took courses at night and during holidays in math and physics education. When Ryan told Amos he was going to university, Amos's first call was to his grandmother.

"When I told her that I'm joining the university this August, she bought me a bag for my books. She had to sell a lot of produce to buy that bag, but she wanted to do it. She is so happy that her grandson is going to college. My grandmother said, 'If I die today, I die a very happy woman.' She keeps asking to see my acceptance letter to confirm that I am going. I have been waiting eight years.

"Ask the girls. When I'm not around, they know I'm at school. They are depending on me to change their situation. What I have failed to do myself, now I can help them do. One day I will prepare someone to go to college."

Ryan and Teka also broke the good news to Claris and Musa that the foundation could pay their tuition for university. After completing her business management degree at the certificate level, Claris decided to go back to school to get a degree in education at the university level. Abdul, her students, and her coworkers are all so proud of her. For Claris, their pride is secondary.

"My mother is so happy," she beamed. For just a moment, she gave a flash of the little girl who played for Girls Soccer in Kibera and clung to her mother on the railroad tracks.

The KGSA Foundation also paid for Linet, Asha, and Lynn to go to college. They were the three who took the initiative to find a school and a program, apply, and approach the foundation for funding. In addition to Violet, KCDF is sponsoring Pauline's post-secondary education.

Teka wanted to go to university himself. And now it was finally his turn too. Ryan told him the foundation was paying for him to go.

"Ryan is the one who made me believe in myself. He has given me hope. He pushed me to go to university. It has been my inner dream. I have never told anyone. Now because of the KGSA Foundation, I am finally going to Nairobi University to get a bachelor's of commerce in finance and accounting."

KGSA soccer was going well. While graduates like Rose and Commando continued to fight for spots on Kenya's National Team, current KGSA student athletes were starting to get plenty of national attention too. Maureen was invited repeatedly to tryouts for national and international tournaments as goalkeeper. The other girl creating quite a buzz was Lucy.

Lucy grew up in rural Kenya, where her parents were farmers and they always had enough food. She taught herself soccer in the wide-open fields. "When I was still in primary school, I started getting involved in soccer, a boy's game. I loved playing with a ball made from disposed paper bags. I played alone. I was never taught how to kick, but I just practiced all day long."

Right before starting sixth grade, Lucy's family moved to Nairobi, and she enrolled at St. John's. After one of her St. John's games, Byrones approached her and asked her if she wanted to play for KGSA's junior team. Desperate to play, she said yes and made the team. After graduating primary school, Lucy started attending KGSA for school too. While playing for KGSA in a tournament in Mombasa, she got noticed by the right people. A man approached her after the tournament and said, "I see something very special in you."

"I did what I do best—play—and it saved me," Lucy said.

In August of 2012, that same man came to KGSA inquiring about Lucy. He invited her to be on the eighteen-and-under national team in Kenya. When there are big, freestanding international tournaments, girls from KGSA like Lucy may be invited to represent Kenya at the tournament. After the tournament, they return to KGSA's eighteen-and-under team.

"It was a dream come true. I had never imagined that I would play for a national team. Byrones helped me with the paper processing and made sure I got everything I needed. The first time we went for training for the national team, I was so excited. I saw many people from different regions in the country assembled together just because of soccer. I felt the power of soccer when we gathered. There was no discrimination, no poor, no rich; we assembled with the same uniform to play for our nation of Kenya."

The coaches from Manchester United were hired to train the girls, and Lucy was starstruck. She loved the training, and the coaches loved her and Maureen. The team manager called Byrones one day during training and said, "You have good players—both in character and skill." Byrones was beaming on the other end of the phone, and told the other KGSA players as encouragement. He knows that both talent and character matter for being chosen for the national teams.

The respect was mutual. Maureen and Lucy leaned on Byrones to help them navigate this new, exciting world. "Byrones went through so much when we were preparing to go to the national competition," Maureen said. "He made sure that no one used our innocence, because we are minors."

At the tournament, Kenya beat Malawi 11-0, Sierra Leone 2-1, and

Burkina Faso 3-0. They lost to Chad in the finals 2-1, but they made a strong showing.

"I get my inspiration from a Kenyan player who plays in France, Dennis Oliech," Maureen said. "He, like me, came from a poor family and had dreams of playing for international teams. I want to play for Spain. The sky's the limit, and in this case, the sky is Spain for me. After graduation, I want to be on the national team to play soccer full time."

Lucy and Maureen, who were getting the attention that Rose and Commando used to get, had an advantage. They were younger, and they benefited from an older KGSA that had wised up to the barriers for female soccer players to make a living in Kenya. As Lucy and Maureen improved in soccer, they also built up their skills and knowledge. They couldn't bank on making it in soccer. KGSA wouldn't let them.

People in the soccer world saw Lucy's raw midfielder talent and work ethic on the field and suggested that she drop school to focus on soccer. She explained that she wanted to be a doctor as well as a soccer player. Her father suffered from an eye disease, and she wanted to help people like him who couldn't afford healthcare. She plaited hair to raise money, and gave any money she made by winning tournaments to her family to help, but she knew she needed more schooling in order to advance in life.

"I need to know how to calculate my money, how to speak English, and also how to express myself in front of people. I need to be extremely educated if I am going to be in the limelight. I will be going for education first."

Lucy also got offers to go to more formal schools with bigger soccer programs to study and train. She always said no. "Abdul is like our father, and Christine guides like a mother. Teka helped me financially when I was applying to play for the national team. Everything I have achieved in the soccer world right now is thanks to this school. I won't leave them."

* * *

At 3:30 p.m. on a Journalism Club day, Asha started setting up Teka's laptop to videoconference with a school in New York. She opened Teka's Skype account, hoping the Internet signal would hold. Asha picked a few girls who were interested in being in on the call. Then they waited. Shortly after 4:00 p.m., they got the call.

The New LIFE School (TNLS) in the South Bronx caters to students who, for any number of reasons, do not excel in the public school system. The parallels between KGSA and TNLS are strong. They both opened in 2006. TNLS had twenty-eight students. They grew, moved twice to a nicer building, and in 2012, served over two hundred students in grades five through twelve.

The school is in a tough neighborhood, and the students struggled with issues like severe learning disabilities and emotional/behavioral disorders. Like KGSA, the school's success did not lie in how many students went on to college. They were trying to keep these students safe and healthy, offering them an alternative to residential facilities and group homes. Vocational training classes assisted students in finding jobs after graduation. The students were proud of not dropping out. And like KGSA, they had recently sent their first student to community college. The schools decided it might be good for students on both ends to reach out across the world to learn from each other.

A select group of students from TNLS sat in desks arranged in a semicircle. The faces of the KGSA students Asha, Dalifa, and Belynder were projected on a wall. It was 9:00 a.m. in the Bronx and 4:00 p.m. in Kibera. Slow Internet in Kibera caused a delay, but the communication between the two communities was strong.

Belynder spoke of getting up at 4:00 a.m. to get her siblings ready for school before the long walk in. She is the firstborn, and her parents' deaths left them orphans. Tyler at TNLS spoke of riding the subway to school, which earned sighs of amazement from the KGSA girls.

They compared phones and discussed *The Twilight Saga*, and whether they preferred Team Edward or Team Jacob. They shared career goals and love of musicians like Chris Brown and Beyoncé.

There are aspects of being a teenager that are universal. Kaitlin asked the Kenyan girls what their Facebook names were so that the cross-cultural conversation could continue. When the call ended, Asha, Dalifa, and Belynder were beaming. "They are so nice! Can we be their friends?" This was their world now. It was normal to chat with new friends in the Bronx on a Friday afternoon with a laptop before heading through the dusty streets toward home.

For Dalifa, it was just the confidence boost she needed with the regional JA Competition approaching on July 14. Ida's crew had gotten fifth place. Asha's earned fourth. The pressure was on Dalifa to lead her team into the top three and onto the Kenya National JA Competition in October.

Teka believed that the Journalism Club was more important than school because students need skills and business sense to set them up for success in either the informal job market of Kibera or the formal job market of Nairobi. The informal market is all about entrepreneurship. If you have electricity, you can make a few shillings by letting people charge their phones. If you have access to watermelons and pineapples, you can sell them by the slice since few can afford to purchase them whole. Creativity abounds, driven by the need to survive. The JA Competition, asking young people to understand and follow through with successful business models at such a young age, was working to set these students up for success.

Dalifa's crew competed against forty-three high schools, including some of the top schools in the country. They were the only school from Kibera. The competition was held at a large, pristine high school campus.

Students got off their buses and were soon busy setting up booths to display their businesses in a large, open field. KGSA came ready with banners, balloons, streamers, brochures, laptops, cameras, and video cameras. They were all dressed in perfect uniforms. The Muslim girls matched in their best white headscarves. It was as heated and well attended as a sports tournament, but the focus was on entrepreneurship.

Teka got off the bus in dressy gray slacks, a purple shirt, and an argyle sweater. It was game time. He admitted that he was nervous, but he did not let the girls sense it. He wanted his students to at least make the top ten so they would have the opportunity to present to the whole group in the auditorium. During the morning setup, no one could find Teka. He stayed away so the girls would not depend on him; he wanted them to know they could do it all on their own.

The Journalism Club at KGSA presented *Shedders* with a few other clubs watching. With the earnings from its magazine and its wedding photo and video business, *Shedders* was able to get a year's supply of clean water for the school and build a hand-washing station. They also contributed to *Global Vantage*, an international youth magazine run out of California. They were focused, poised, and professional. The club officers passed out their brochures, annual report, and business plan to the judges and presented different aspects of *Shedders* with the support of PowerPoint in a timed talk. They were named in the top ten, requiring them to present to a new panel in the large auditorium open to everyone.

Midday at the JA Competition, Abdul showed up with lunch for the girls. Kids from other schools bought their lunch at the canteen. KGSA girls did not have the money to do that. In a bright yellow T-shirt and Nike baseball cap, Abdul crossed the field toward the KGSA booth with bags of food. The girls took a break and made a circle in the grass for their picnic lunch. Abdul watched like a proud father.

"I love seeing our girls out of Kibera. It's in moments like these when I can really see that we are a family. Look at them sharing food, playing with each other's hair. It's just lovely."

After lunch, he went around to all the other booths, encouraging the other students too. When he came back, he said matter-of-factly, "There are some interesting ideas, but our business is the strongest. If you present well, you can win."

Abdul noticed the girls stayed closer to each other than most of the other schools. "Girls in other schools were reaching out to boys. Our girls were there with a purpose. During the last minutes, when the last schools were performing, most of these other schools had gone out and were sitting and playing. Our girls were really listening and learning. They sat there and saw the people who defeated them and the people they defeated. It will help them in their fight. They showed a lot of maturity. They showed respect for each other."

Dalifa admitted to being nervous for the final round and feeling sick when they took the stage, but no one could tell. She took three deep breaths before leading her team onstage. She started their presentation with a quote, confidently projected to the crowd: "You cannot resist change, but you can influence it."

The group had to wait to continue, smiling, until the applause for Dalifa's opening died down. Then each minister of the company presented their information on finances, human resources, and marketing, slides included, without referring to notes. Habiba, the only first-year student onstage, slipped up just a bit, but recovered nicely.

Teka whispered, "I told her to stare at their foreheads so she wouldn't get nervous. But she is so young. She has time."

The girls finished presenting to the panel of judges in the time allotted and walked in single file off the stage to their folding chairs in the front. Abdul was pleased.

"Their presentation was more than I expected," he said. "They stood up onstage in front of hundreds of students. Dalifa started it on a different note. She was the only person applauded at the start of the presentation. They knew the vision. They knew the mission. Not like other students referring to notes. Our girls had everything by head and by heart."

Nine hours after the competition started, *Shedders* of KGSA was named third in the competition, earning them their first-ever invitation to the national competition. As the president, Dalifa, went onstage to collect her trophy, the Journalism Club erupted in screams of happiness and celebration.

After the award ceremony, the top ten businesses were invited up onstage to get door prizes. When the JA deejay started the music, a spontaneous dance party erupted on the auditorium stage. Teka and Abdul watched the girls laugh and dance from the audience. The celebration for the girls felt monumental and multilayered. They had worked so hard, and the victory was not just about the trophy. A young man from a top-ten school, tall and broad-shouldered in his uniform, started dancing toward Marci, a stunning KGSA Journalism Club member. He had made eye contact with her and was approaching her with a swagger, leading with his hips. The KGSA girls noticed the approach and saw Marci's eyes darting around uncomfortably. Without missing a beat, ten girls danced in to surround her. They laughed and screamed as Dalifa raised the trophy over her head, and they all exited the stage together.

Teka said, "I'm so proud of the girls, but I haven't told them that yet. If I tell them they are good, they are going to relax. The competition is not over. We need to win nationals, to show Kenya what the girls from Kibera can do. When *Shedders* goes to compete, I don't think about what position they will get, but being able to tell the story of Kibera the best. When people hear Kibera, they don't expect what our girls show them.

"At the competition, my main photographer was jockeying for positions with the adult photographers at the event. We go to these big functions, and I don't touch the cameras. They can take good photos, but they need to be fearless.

"Our girls were competing against the best and biggest schools in Kenya. We can beat them in soccer, in the JA Competition, in drama, in science. Why can't we beat them in the KCSE?"

On the bus ride through Nairobi, the girls sang the whole way. When the bus turned into Kibera, their volume seemed to double as if they were announcing, "We are home." People in Kibera now know about KGSA. They, too, are proud of the trophies the girls bring back into the slum. The girls feel like winners. They know they belong.

Instead of being annoyed at the ruckus, Abdul smiled. "That's their pride. They're just kids. Let them play. Let them be."

★ ★ ★

Zakiya and Abdul celebrated their nine-year anniversary and mourned nine years of trying to have a child with no success. "People started putting pressure on Abdul to take another wife," Zakiya said. "They called me barren. I cried when I saw my menses. Nothing. Nothing. It was hard. All my friends had children. I went from hospital to hospital, but they all said there was nothing wrong."

Then Zakiya started feeling nauseated. Her friends and even her house help noticed that her breasts were getting bigger. But she had given up hope. "Those things happened before my menses too. I refused to go to the hospital because I didn't want to get disappointed." Zakiya did, however, let her friend take a urine sample to the hospital.

She called screaming, "Zakiya! It's positive! You're pregnant!"

In disbelief, Zakiya went to three different clinics to make sure. She held the secret inside for two days. On Abdul's forty-second birthday, she told him, "I have a gift for you." She placed an envelope on the table with results signed by the doctor inside.

Abdul sat down on the couch across from Zakiya and opened the envelope. "What? Is it true?" he sank back into the couch. Sobbing, he told her, "This is the best gift I have ever received."

A few months later, Zakiya and Abdul found out they were going to have a baby boy.

BURNING BRIGHTER
2013

Hurry, hurry has no blessing.

—SWAHILI PROVERB

In 2009, Abdul symbolically handed the school over to Teka. Busy at Stichting 4 Life, he would ask Teka, "How's your school doing?" Abdul taught Teka how to talk to donors and make strategic, rational decisions. He taught Teka how to trust.

"People in Kibera assume I am Nubian and Muslim because Abdul and I get along so well. He is my role model." The power that Abdul handed over to Teka, Teka handed over to Freidah, Musa, Claris, and Amos as KGSA continued to grow and he got busier with college classes of his own.

Principal Christine left KGSA after the 2012 school year. Teka and Abdul approached Freidah, a teacher, about the position. She had a college degree, was reliable and committed to the girls, and they wanted to keep a woman in that leadership role. She was surprised, but she accepted the promotion. She worked hard, earned the trust of the girls, and was great at goal-setting and training teachers. The third-year students that year were notorious for misbehaving, so she focused on discipline and classroom performance.

In the 2012 KCSE exam, five girls failed math compared to eleven in 2011, and one KGSA student earned an A in math for the first time. Two girls scored high enough for degree work and another six earned the C necessary for diploma work. Out of the thirty-seven secondary schools in the area, KGSA scored twenty-third on the KCSE. Slowly, there were glimpses of academic improvement despite the struggle to carve out study time for the students and the challenges of teacher retention.

Freidah said, "We're doing well considering what our girls are up against. Our top girl, Mary, was living with her uncle in a violent neighborhood. He worked nights as a watchman, leaving her vulnerable and alone. She developed ulcers from the stress, so we had her move in with a teacher. But we cannot take all the girls in to live with us, so we must keep working to make their home lives stable enough for them to be able to study."

Retaining good teachers, especially qualified female teachers and science teachers, continued to be a struggle. Their 15,000-shilling monthly salary couldn't compete with other schools. That wasn't enough money for a woman to buy food for her family, and it was culturally still the job of the woman to provide food.

A third hindrance to academic performance at KGSA had been a lack of access to information. Then one strategic and generous donation helped. In December of 2012, Teka got an email from World-reader. After reading an article about KGSA by a Journalism Club member in *Global Vantage*, an anonymous donor in California raised money to donate 100 e-readers through Worldreader to KGSA. In February of 2013 when the e-readers arrived, Teka took a taxi to the airport without really understanding what an e-reader was or how it worked. He invited a few girls to come to the school and help him unpack the three boxes he picked up.

"When I held the e-reader in my hand, then I understood," he said. "The girls were so excited. They said, 'These are for us? Now we are going to pass with flying colors.' The e-readers can hold 3,000 books. Instead of carrying heavy bags around, they just have one light device."

They installed syllabus books, a dictionary, the Bible, the Koran, study tools for the KCSE, educational games, and storybooks. Teka trained the teachers and prefects in the library before spending a day training all the girls. At the end of the training, KGSA invited families to a ceremony to launch the e-reader program so that the whole community would help care for the devices. Community partners like Alla Vida, board members, and friends of Worldreader also came. The donors were there, but they did not want to say anything or be recognized.

Abdul said, "This reminded me that there are good people out there who have a lot of money. We just need to reach them with our story."

There was music and soda. A few girls recited poems and danced. The Worldreader employees gave a speech. The parents signed an agreement to help care for the devices, and a few parents spoke.

Worldreader recommended not allowing the girls to bring the devices home. They told KGSA to keep the e-readers at school to avoid them being broken or stolen. But the teachers explained to Worldreader that the girls are in class all day. To benefit fully from the devices, they had to take them home to study. KGSA gave out twenty of the e-readers over the Easter holiday. All twenty came back on time in perfect condition.

"We have not had any cases of breakage," Teka reported. "It's a sophisticated device and people respect the girls for having it. They would rather talk to her about it than steal it. The girls share with their siblings and neighbors. They teach their parents how to use them. The girls love Sudoku and math games, and the reading culture has really improved. They love to read."

Before the e-reader, 130 girls had to share the out-of-date books in the library. With one hundred e-readers, more girls had access to the materials they needed to learn. Principal Freidah was excited to see how the e-readers could improve classroom performance. The struggles, however, remained the same. Many KGSA students didn't have enough time to study at home because of chores, fetching water, and lack of privacy and electricity.

Teka downloaded his college books onto one and used it to become a better chemistry teacher. It also changed the learning culture in Kibera. Several community members came by KGSA, curious about the e-readers after seeing them in the community. KGSA opened its library to nonstudents, letting the e-readers be used on campus by anyone who wanted to read.

In May of 2013, David Risher, the cofounder of Worldreader, came to see KGSA. Teka and Amos took him to the homes of a few students in fairly unsafe neighborhoods at his request. Later during David's visit when he spoke to the vice president of Kenya, William Ruto, he recommended that more politicians visit Kibera in general and KGSA specifically.

For years, girls in the Journalism Club have submitted quarterly articles to the Global Journal Project. They were published in *Global Vantage Magazine*, which hoped to connect international communities through story sharing. The donation for the e-readers came from one eighteen-year-old boy who read an article about KGSA and was inspired to raise funds. His parents contributed a matching gift. The story came full circle in the summer of 2013. KGSA downloaded *Global Vantage* on their e-readers. Sheriffar Jaffar and Lilian Agui wrote poems that were published in the magazine. They sat in amazement, reading their own poems on the new e-readers.

While e-readers were good news for the girls' minds, 2013 also brought good news for the girls' bodies. For years, KGSA relied on donors and organizations like CARE to provide menstrual pads for the girls. KGSA partnered with Ruby Cup to work on a more sustainable option. Ruby Cup is a silicone product that women wear internally while menstruating. Lasting for ten years, it is a one-time purchase that is kind to the environment and the budget. The company started in Denmark. The price of a Ruby Cup online is determined such that a part of the proceeds can keep the price of Ruby Cups low in Kenya. Ryan did a simple Facebook campaign to raise the 700 shillings, eight U.S. dollars, per Ruby Cup necessary to offer one to any KGSA girl who was interested. Ruby Cup employees Maximilla and Rowena came to KGSA for orientation wearing pink Ruby Cup T-shirts that said, "No wings or strings attached." Some of the girls were nervous about the idea of insertion, but one KGSA student admitted to already using one. It had taken time to get the hang of, but she liked it. She helped her classmates consider the possibility, and over 100 students decided to get one. Julie, the founder of Ruby Cup, said, "Usually girls in Kenya are skeptical at first. It just takes one brave girl to say she'll try it, and then the rest of the girls know they will figure it out together."

Principal Freidah recommended that the program be opened to friends and family as well. "The girls share everything. When we give them pads, they usually share a few with moms and sisters because they are so expensive. We don't want the girls sharing their Ruby Cups for sanitary reasons, so we have to offer it to everyone."

When the Ruby Cup team came to KGSA to do training, the male teachers stayed in the library, but their interest was piqued too. Sam stood reading a pink promotional poster and asked Ryan, "These really last for ten years? So if I get one for my sister, I won't have to buy her pads for a decade?"

KGSA held the Ruby Cup distribution at school on a Saturday. The girls split up into their classrooms and Ruby Cup employees started with a little lesson on female sexual and reproductive anatomy. The girls shouted out the names of the different orifices on cue, "Rectum! Urethra! Vagina!" Some girls were concerned that using the Ruby Cup would somehow interfere with their virginity. Talking about menstrual hygiene was a natural way to do essential sex education too. At one distribution, a girl asked a Ruby Cup team member what she should do if a man tries to rape her while she has the Ruby Cup in. The team member took her time answering, addressing the question at the body level and also how she can seek help and advocate for herself as a victim of assault.

Each participating student took a pink box with a Ruby Cup and a cloth bag, a flyer, an instruction packet, a small bucket, and sanitation tablets to clean the cup between periods. They practiced folding the cup together. There were a few nervous giggles. Lillian, a third-year student, admitted, "I'm afraid it's going to hurt. I think I'll wait for my friends to try it first. If it works for them, then I'll try it."

Maureen chimed in, "Yeah I'm scared of trying something new, but we're going to do it together as a family. That makes me feel braver."

Ruby Cup came just in time. Freidah was all too aware of the empty corner in her office that normally housed menstrual pads. With the Ruby Cup partnership, Freidah saved time trying to find pad donors and money.

It was a big year for Dalifa. She and her Journalism Club comrades attended the JA National Competition gala at the InterContinental Hotel, one of the most prestigious hotels in Kenya. The girls enjoyed a five-course meal. They asked Teka what all the cutlery was for and were amazed that each hotel room had a television with over 100 channels. They were not too starstruck, however, to lose sight of the mission to shed light on what it means to be a girl in Kibera.

Dalifa said, "We talked to people who had never heard of Kibera and explained our products to them well, in English, a language we like using to show that we are educated. We stood in front of people who see bad pictures of Kibera in the news. We wanted to disprove the myth that people from the slums cannot do anything productive in life. Before the competition, I visited the principal's office to see the cup we won at the Nairobi competition. We waited for the opportunity to go to Nationals for years."

They placed in the top sixteen.

In February, she got her KCSE test results back. She made her uncle look at the score first because she was so nervous. When she saw him smile, she grabbed her phone and screamed. Dalifa, scoring sixty-five points, became the first KGSA graduate to score a B on her exam and qualify for a government scholarship to college. Shaking with excitement, Dalifa had her sister call her mother to share the good news. "I made my mother happy and proud of me. When I go to university, when I get a job, when I help her, she will smile, and I will be happy."

Dalifa worked at KGSA as a lab assistant while awaiting her acceptance letter to university. She replaced Lynn, who was studying in post-secondary school. Her classmate Belynder got a B−, just missing a scholarship by a few points. The KGSA Foundation paid her tuition at Kenyatta University where she studied secondary education in biology and chemistry. She became KGSA's librarian. With the help of her church and a continued connection with Anne Baldwin, Ida started taking classes as well.

Of the thirty who took the KCSE exam, ten scored a C− or higher. While that number crept higher every year, KGSA offered more and more support for the girls not going on to post-secondary education. Teka was awarded a large grant from KCDF to do business training for graduates. He invited every graduate of KGSA to attend. Forty came, and at the end, ten were awarded microloans to start small businesses. Judy was one of the ten graduates granted a loan. A 2009 graduate, she opened a small stand along the railroad track selling shoes from nine to six every day with the exception of a short lunch break.

"I can't complain," she said, sitting on a stool next to a rickety table piled high with jelly shoes in clear plastic wrapping. "The neighbors are nice. I'm grateful for the loan. The shoes sell well."

Her rent for the stand was 1,500 shillings a month, with shoes selling for around 200 shillings a pair. She picked up a pair of children's shoes, Crocs knockoffs with Spider-man on them. After paying rent, her proceeds went toward her diabetes medication and food. Other graduates put their loans toward salons or stands selling *kangas*, groceries, or second hand clothes.

The exciting partnership with and funding from KCDF (the

organization that gave money for the tie-dying initiative in 2006 and funded *Shedders'* new journalism studio) and Alla Vida (an organization helping with food, soccer expenses, and lab chemicals) stopped abruptly. Due to changes in legislation, the two organizations were prohibited from funneling foreign money into Kenyan organizations without going through the Finance Ministry. Other partnerships, however, grew stronger. For example, Denver University, which originally started a partnership with KGSA in 2010, worked toward having an internship component in their School of Social Work program, which provided counseling to students at the school.

And the Stichting 4 Life connection continued. John and Linda were very active in Kibera, running the beading company, supporting eighty students, and buying property for primary schools. For KGSA, they also provided some money for the food budget. Additionally, they helped four graduates get jobs at a flower farm outside of Nairobi. Mercy, one of the KGSA graduates accepted at the farm, worked hard from nine to four every day packaging gorgeous flowers while wearing a one-piece jumpsuit and big rubber boots. The farm shipped 250,000 flowers a week all over the world. When demand was low, they sold in Kenya. The flowers needed to get into the trucks by three every afternoon to make it to the airport on time. The packaging room was kept cold, and Mercy sported a wool cap to stay warm. She lived in a small home with the other three KGSA graduates who worked at the farm. They slept in one room to save money so they could send more funds home. She made 8,000 shillings a month. After life in Kibera, nights were eerily quiet there.

"I miss home," she said, "but I have to raise money to send my siblings to school."

Beatrice and Jacqueline worked in the administrative office in sales and human resources respectively. There were 755 employees on the farm. The girls spoke well of Kibera and KGSA despite being made fun of. Jacqueline liked her office work and hoped to be a manager someday. Beatrice spoke to clients from Holland, Japan, and Russia who sent pictures of bruised flowers and wanted rebates. She missed the

Poetry Club at KGSA, so she approached her boss about writing poems about flowers they could attach to the shipments. "No matter what I do in life, I want to always add value. I want to insert beauty where I can."

When the girls got discouraged while waiting for promotions that would give them more than entry-level salaries, the Stichting 4 Life staff encouraged them to take certificate courses to strengthen their résumés. It was easy for them to feel stuck and isolated on the farm.

Back in Kibera, Asha excelled at Moi University, studying journalism, community development, and criminology. In addition to helping with the Journalism Club and the KGSA Foundation, she got an internship at Pamoja FM 99.9, "The Voice of Kibera." The radio station was started in 2007 by USAID after the postelection violence. On the third floor in the middle of Kibera, Asha had a bird's-eye view of the slum. From her vantage point, she could see the mosque, tin roofs, blue buses, and women washing clothes. Pamoja sent Asha out to conduct interviews. She learned how to write scripts and cut tapes to make tight radio sound bites.

On Fridays during Ramadan, when Pamoja dedicates the whole day's programming to Muslims, Asha was allowed to queue up Islamic music and assist as an imam took questions from listeners about the compulsory giving of alms to the poor. She got up at four to be at the station by six. The power was out; the station used a generator. The room with foam walls and an egg-carton ceiling was dark. She sat on the left of the small On-Air room. One hand was on a red phone; the other was on a blue Koran.

After the imam left, Asha took over temporarily. She put the earphones on, flipped a switch, and said with clear confidence to the caller, "This is Asha Jaffar, and you are on Pamoja 99.9." While Muslim songs played on air, she blasted pop songs internally, singing along loudly. She fluctuated rapidly between being silly and being serious.

Asha's poetry was gaining publicity through the Kenya Poetry Lounge, and she received the Haller Prize for Development Journalism. After finishing two years of diploma work at Moi, she was ready to start her two years of degree work at university.

"I am going to take community development and social work classes in college so that I can learn how to manage an organization and look for funds. I really want to help Abdul and KGSA."

KGSA had become more than a school. Abdul, Teka, and Ryan were slowly trying to change the identity of KGSA to convey what it had become: a three-pronged community organization that supports young women through (1) a free secondary school, (2) a rigorous and successful community sports program, and (3) a microfinance program for parents, graduates, and community members, with vocational and job-skills training. They believed these three efforts would provide space for women to excel and change the perception of where a woman's place is in society, while keeping young women safe and empowered.

As KGSA evolved, the board needed to grow as well. It was Alla Vida that originally put pressure on Abdul and Teka to form a board. Abdul admitted, "It was hard to hand my baby over to other people." The first board was a bit makeshift; attendance and commitment were low in part because the board was international. Abdul started over, making a local board that could help KGSA become more professional, with a constitution, strategic plan, monitoring and evaluation, and governance and policies. With these structures in place, KGSA would be eligible for more funding and would build trust with more philanthropic organizations. Abdul knew that KGSA had outgrown him, and he was relieved to have a professional, committed board to create legitimacy, fundraise for Kenyan money, and support him. The board included a pilot, a human-resources manager, and a business owner, as well as Jeffrey, KGSA's first teacher, Fred from Sporting Chance, Dr. Jama, and Patrick Omutia, the secretary of sports, arts and culture in the Kenyan Parliament. The board paid to have all the stakeholders—KGSA teachers, students, strategic alumni, and soccer players—meet for a two-day brainstorming session. From that meeting, a forty-page document was created that the board edited into KGSA's strategic plan. Abdul's commitment to putting the girls at the center of change continued. "The board puts on suits and goes out for me to find Kenyan money," he said. "They track donors and thank them. This will work. New partners make the fire brighter. Slowly by slowly, we are getting brighter. We are here to stay."

In the midst of Abdul's professional growth, he prepared for his family to grow too. During Zakiya's pregnancy, the doctors told her that her body was producing too much amniotic fluid. The risk involved the baby ingesting too much fluid. They said that if she could carry the baby to eight months, he would be viable, and they would do a cesarean section. She went to the clinic twice a month, which was expensive for Abdul at 6,000 shillings a visit. Her belly grew. They waited, counting the days.

In her seventh month, Zakiya made Abdul feel her stomach. "He's not moving, Abdul," she said. "I haven't felt him move today."

She went in for an ultrasound. She called from the hospital. "They are saying my baby's dead. Our baby is dead."

"I'm coming."

The doctors warned against inducing her, so they decided on the more expensive option of surgically removing the baby. Students from KGSA came to the hospital to surround Zakiya. Teka and other staff and friends came to support Abdul.

Zakiya and Abdul named the boy Iman, which means belief. While she recovered, Abdul took Iman home, washed him, and buried him. At three in the morning, after he buried the baby, Abdul returned to the hospital to cry with Zakiya.

"All these old mommas came from the Nubian community to comfort me. They told me stories of women who waited years to get pregnant, lost children, and now had houses full of kids," Abdul said. "So many people came with me to bury the baby. In Kibera, people come out for you."

Zakiya took the loss hard. She wouldn't leave the house. She didn't want to see anybody. The gossip continued, and people continued to put pressure on Abdul to take a second wife.

By Ramadan, however, she opened her home up to family and

friends to break the fast together. She invited students and Abdul's nineteen-year-old daughter from a previous relationship over to cook for Abdul's friends. Abdul's daughter was studying international relations and Chinese in part because of Abdul and Zakiya's support over the years. "We are not a closed family. Zakiya is good at surrounding herself with people who become family. There are always kids running around, KGSA students calling her 'Mom.' It makes the healing easier," Abdul said. "But we want our own family."

Zakiya got up at three in the morning to say an extra prayer at the mosque during Ramadan. They are hopeful.

Since GSK started in 2002 and KGSA opened in 2006, Abdul has invited foreigners to come see for themselves what he was doing. KGSA's most dedicated partners tend to be people who have spent significant time at the school. More recently, KGSA folks have been invited to do the traveling. Out of forty applicants, the Human Needs Project chose to fly Byrones to San Francisco for leadership training. He extended his trip to meet some of KGSA's main supporters across the United States and flourished while there. Abdul said, "I am so proud of Byrones. He's so smart and charismatic. He has admitted his mistakes and is growing so fast." After KGSA hosted a teacher and a few students from Denmark in an exchange program, Lucy and Amos were invited to go to Denmark in 2014.

After trips to the United Kingdom with Sporting Chance and the Netherlands through Stichting 4 Life and years of trying to get a travel visa to the United States, Abdul was granted access to the U.S., and the foundation planned a cross-country, five-week tour for him. He met supporters, spoke at meetings and dinners, won new donors, and built new strategic partnerships in California, Colorado, Minnesota, Massachusetts, New York, and Washington, D.C. The main purpose of the tour was to raise money for the Elevate Education Campaign, the proceeds of which went toward building KGSA's dormitory. After thirty-five days, nine cities, sixty-seven meetings, four college visits, thirteen events, five high school visits, and eleven different beds, Abdul and Ryan raised over $100,000, with more funds committed for the future. The dormitory budget was $300,000, which was becoming an attainable goal.

Design Source, a Kenyan architectural firm, agreed to take Mookie's design and build it. Agreeing to work pro bono to advise and connect with affordable contractors, Design Source saved KGSA $40,000. The next step in the campaign was that U.S. supporters, each raising $10,000, climbed Mount Kilimanjaro. The organization 1,000 Shades of Green outfitted the climb free of cost so the proceeds raised could go straight to the dormitory budget. The owner, Morgan, had studied under Ryan's father at college in the U.S. Before moving back to Africa to start his business, Morgan and Ryan had connected. The climb guaranteed that the dormitory would become a reality.

"The KGSA Foundation has made Teka and me more daring and focused," Abdul said. "They are always willing to pay our running costs like teachers' salaries. The dormitory was a long shot, but with the foundation, we did it. Ryan and I are brothers. It has been a great connection.

"Westerners say, 'We have everything, but we still want more.' They are not even happy. In Kibera, we love our music loud. We laugh loudly. We shake hands vigorously. There is spice in life. Kids play on a heap of dirt. We hope. We live on hope in Kibera, hoping tomorrow will be better. That hope creates positivity.

"Maybe that is God's way. 'I won't give you everything. I will give you Westerners money and a little happiness, and I will give you Kiberans hope.' Then maybe these two meet and create something beautiful together."

Back in 2006, Abdul would stop by Salim's brother's house to make sure young Teka was doing okay and that the soccer players were safe, fed, and learning. By 2013, he would check in on the HIV-positive mothers beading in the morning, swing by the primary school he sponsors before lunch, and sit in KGSA's library, finally full of books and computers, in the afternoon. He did a crossword puzzle while

Teka started the Journalism Club meeting, Byrones walked the soccer team to the bus, and the prefects coordinated after-school cleaning.

He remembered every grant, donation, and addition to the school building, staff, and programming, growing as a leader with each success. The immediate work required him to strategize about expanding the clubs, improving test performance, strengthening the microfinance system, training the teachers, and building a dormitory. It was exciting work, and Abdul was present for it. Yet his sights were simultaneously set on the bigger picture, the longer view. It always was that way. Learning from the past and engaging in the present informed his dreams of the future. The vision is clear. He believes that the same little girls who were scared to go on the soccer field with the boys will one day be running KGSA.

"Everybody has a purpose in life. Maybe KGSA is what my purpose has been," Abdul said. "Given another chance, I would go back and do the same thing all over again. All the positive things in my life came from women—my mother, my grandmother, and my aunts. The school is my way of giving back. Seeing these girls blossom is payment enough. They come to school timid. The first year, they start whispering. The second year, they start talking. The third year, they start yelling. The fourth year, they put their heads down to study for their exams. It is beautiful. We have not gone the full cycle, but we are close now with girls going to university.

"I can walk away from KGSA when, slowly by slowly, we have a dorm, a soccer field, and more graduates going to university. We are already seeing positive—not tangible, but positive—successes in the way the girls look at issues in life. Linet wants to become a teacher. Dalifa wants to run the school. I encourage it. They know the bounty will come to them. It would be lovely to hand it over to them. I will sit on the board and be lazy and wait to have a meeting with them every three months. Dalifa, Linet, Asha, and Lynn can run the school. That would be outstanding. There is the family at work. Very soon, they will be running their own show."

Dalifa likes Abdul's plan. It fits with hers. "I want to study education and teach math and chemistry at KGSA. I want to stay in Kibera to change it, and it will start by educating the girls. The more educated the people are, the more innovative we become, the better Kibera gets.

"Abdul is my role model. I would be glad to take over Girls Soccer when he needs me. Then I can help the girls the way he helped me. I pray to God to give him a long life to enjoy. I know right now he is worrying so much about the girls. I just want God to give him a peaceful life. We have to come back and take over so he can rest. He is a good man."

The girls crowded the library. Some played Scrabble. Others practiced "Hot Cross Buns" on the keyboard that Ryan had donated. At the four working computers, girls sat on each other's laps or hooked their chins over each other's shoulders so everyone could see the screens. The Internet was working that day. They took turns checking Facebook and reading blogs. It was an August morning—nearly the end of the second term. Teachers sat in the lounge correcting papers and calculating scores. Exams went well. The teachers were in high spirits. On Friday, there would be a celebration, regardless of results. The top three in each class would receive small prizes. The graduate interns would take turns offering words of encouragement to the current students.

"Work hard."

"Stay away from boys."

"Focus on your dreams."

"Look at me. I came from nothing. I passed, and now I am working. If I can do it, so can you."

Rice and beans were served for lunch. Some of the girls had a few extra shillings and ran around the corner to buy avocados. The girls who finished first moved to the water station to clean their plates and hands. Then they set up an intricate game of dodge ball in the broom-swept dirt courtyard. The slower eaters stood on the outskirts and leaned on the walls. They offered an occasional friendly taunt to the girls playing the game.

The Muslim girls grabbed stools from the lab and carried them around the corner to an open space away from the game of dodge ball. Normally, lunch break was not separated by religion, but during Ramadan, they separated because they were fasting. They chatted and giggled, shared lip gloss, and strolled to the mosque for afternoon prayer. They coordinated their head coverings—that day, their scarves were black.

By the time the Muslim girls returned from the mosque, all of the bowls were clean and the impromptu dodge ball game had wound down. Without any instruction from the adults, the girls separated into their individual classrooms. Each of the grades was tasked with creating a performance for Friday's second-term closing ceremony. The first-year students needed a little help from their class teacher, Godwin. They huddled around him and brainstormed ideas for a skit, talking over each other and letting their energy swell to chaos. The second-year students had selected a few representatives to sing a song and others to recite poetry. The third-year students had borrowed Teka's laptop and were arguing over what song to choreograph a dance to. Three girls shook their hips to a techno piece before scrunching their faces in unison and requesting something else.

The fourth-year students' rehearsal was running smoothly. They had done this before and knew how to work well together. One young woman offered her phone to play music on. They decided to use a traditional Luo song. There were eight Luo girls in fourth year, and they stood up in front of the class together working out the details of the dance. The other girls slouched in their desks and relaxed into the repetitive music. They leaned their faces on their fists and watched their friends dance. Smiles gradually spread on their faces. Each time the dance was finished, a girl or two from the desks offered a suggestion or observation, and the eight Luo girls started again from the top.

The dancers had serious, straight faces. They had complete control over their bodies. Their hips moved in rhythm with the repetitive, tribal music. Their movements were strong and sensual, yet unassuming. Violet wandered into the room and leaned against the back wall. She smiled, and her hips started moving in unison with the girls. The blackboard behind the dancers was almost clean. In the upper right corner, it said, "88 Days Left." This was the countdown to the KCSE exam. Some of the girls in the room would fail the KCSE. Some would pass, but not with high-enough marks to get a college scholarship. For those girls, their education might be finished. They would go back into the world to look for jobs or start families. Some of those who passed would be accepted and given scholarships to continue on in college. For all the girls in the room, the future was still unknown. The test haunted them all, as a turning point in their lives that they had been working toward for four years. They wanted, hoped, and prayed to perform well and pass. They believed their futures depended on it. They did. The countdown loomed over them. It was coming, but it was not there yet. That day, they danced.

EPILOGUE

2014–2016

In 2014, the class average of graduates went up an entire letter grade.

Asha, Lynn, Violet, Beattrice, Claris, Amos, Teka, Musa, and Samuel have graduated from college. Linet and Dalifa are in their final year.

In 2014, KGSA was selected as one of the first thirteen Ashoka Changemaker Schools in East Africa, the only one in Nairobi. These schools support children as change makers—individuals with the skill set and connection to purpose that enable them to take initiatives to solve problems and drive positive change in their communities.

The Journalism Club was awarded the Uzuri Award at the 2015 JA Company Challenge. Five students were awarded partial scholarships to Nairobi's Institute of Technology.

In 2016, the dormitory land was cleare for construction. KGSA partnered with Orkidstudio, a sustainable architecture firm, to manage the construction of the dormitory, set to begin in September 2017.

Teka married and had a son, named Rayyan after Ryan Sarafolean.

John Schut of Stichting 4 Life died in November 25, 2015, of cancer. Abdul took it very hard.

In January of 2016, a KGSA soccer player named Kalete died of severe malaria and typhoid, a humbling reminder of the vulnerability of the girls in Kibera. In 2016, with Sean Rush's support, KGSA partnered with a local health clinic to provide students with primary healthcare services including biannual wellness exams, immunizations, and screening for STIs.

Asha, a journalist and a poet, is currently working on documentary on women in Africa. She lives on her own and is helping her family cement their house. In 2016, she traveled to Denmark and in 2017 started her own organization working with girls and women in media.

On April 1, 2016, Ryan Sarafolean stepped down as Executive Director and joined the board, and Shannon Murphy started as the director of the KGSA Foundation. Sean Rush also took a position on the board.

Abdul has decided to run for office. He is vying for a position as Member of Parliament for the Kibera Constituency.

RESOURCES

To Learn More, Go To:

KGSA Foundation: www.kgsafoundation.org

1,000 Shades of Green: www.gogreensafari.com

Alla Vida: www.allavida.org

Awaken Kibera: www.awakenkibera.com

CARE: www.care.org

Carolina for Kibera: www.cfk.unc.edu

Comic Relief: www.comicrelief.com

Geo Girls: http: www.nycgrassrootsmedia.org/node/1340, www.girlville.info/geo

Girl Up: www.girlup.org

The Global Journalism Project: vantage.thegjp.org, www.thegjp.org

Groundwork Opportunities: www.groundoworkopportunities.org

Hearts on Fire: www.heartsonfire.org

Human Needs Project: www.humanneedsproject.org

The Humanitarian News and Analysis Service of the UN Office for the Coordination of Humanitarian Affairs: www.irinnews.org/pdf/nairobi_inventory.pdf

Junior Achievement: www.ja.org

Kenya Community Development Foundation (KCDF): www.kcdf.or.ke

The Lunchbox Fund: www.thelunchboxfund.org

Mag Cloud: www.magcloud.com

Minnesota Studies in International Studies (MSID): www.umabroad.umn.edu

Organic Health Response: www.organichealthresponse.org

Programmes d'Aide et de Développement destinés aux Enfants du Monde (PADEM): www.padem.org

Ruby Cup: www.ruby-cup.com

Seeds for Hope: seedsforhope.org

"Slum Schoolgirls Living the Digital Dream," *Daily Nation*:
www.nation.co.ke

Sporting Chance: www.sportingchanceinternational.org

Stichting 4 Life: www.stichting4life.nl/english

Teach a Man to Fish: www.teachamantofish.org.uk

UNICEF: pdf.usaid.gov/pdf_docs/PNADT495.pdf

University of Denver School of Social Work: www.du.edu/socialwork

World Education: www.worlded.org

Worldreader: www.worldreader.org

Watch:

JA Worldwide, *JA 100 Lives—Richard Teka*: www.youtube.com

Kenya Citizen TV, *Strength of a Woman: Kibera Girls Soccer Academy*:
www.youtube.com

KSTP-TV, *On the Road with Jason Davis—KGSA on the Road*:
www.kstp.com

One World TV, *Slum Survivors*: www.youtube.com

Pulitzer Center, *Water is Life: Women and Water in the Kibera Slum*:
www.kgsafoundation.org

Richard E. Robbins, *Girl Rising*: www.girlrising.com

Robert Gooding, *Kibera Girls Soccer Academy*: www.youtube.com

Seeds For Hope, *You Might Think: Drama for Life*:
www.seedsforhope.com

TEDTalentSearch, *Abdul Kassim: Real Change Requires Listening*:
www.youtube.com

Worldreader, *Learning Curve: Introduction of E-reader at Kibera Girls
Soccer Academy*: www.youtube.com

Read:

The Beautiful Tree

Behind the Beautiful Forevers

Half the Sky

*I am Malala: The Girl Who Stood Up for Education and was Shot by the
Taliban*

It Happened on the Way to War
It's Our Turn to Eat
Kenya: Between Hope and Despair, 1963–2011Planet of Slums
Poor Economics: A Radical Rethinking of the Way to Fight Global Poverty

ACKNOWLEDGMENTS

Many writers equate writing a book with birthing a child. I find this comparison accurate and helpful. In the same way that your child does not actually belong to you, this book is not completely mine. I cared for it and nurtured it for years, as a labor of love, building new scaffolding and fretting over commas. In that way alone, my name is on the cover. But the story lives beyond us, beautiful because of the life breathed into it by oh so many people.

To Daniel, my love, my birthing partner, thank you for being the one to walk with me, sentence by sentence and draft after draft. Your presence was your love. It held me together.

Ryan Sarafolean told me this story first, in a way that shot straight from his heart into mine. I couldn't turn away. He would become my companion and advocate as the story emerged over the following years. Thank you for everything from getting me to and around Kibera to being the first call I wanted to make with good news about the book. Your passion and positivity light the world.

The faculty, staff, and students at KGSA are the heroes of this story. They were so generous with their time, trusting a young, unknown writer from the U.S. from the very first moment. Special thanks go to Asha Jaffar. This book would not exist without you. Thank you for translating, literally and figuratively, for being vulnerable with me and caring about me as a person as well as a writer. You are talented beyond measure. Thank you, Abdul, for making time for me and entrusting the story of your school to me. Your vision matches your compassion and commitment to women. The world needs more men like you. Teka, thank you for making me laugh. Thank you for your patience and kindness. It was an inspiration to walk alongside you in Kibera. Thank you also to everyone in Kibera who offered their time and stories, especially Claris, Zakiya, Byrones, Amos, Musa, Christine, Freidah, Faridah, Dr. Jama, Godwin, Samuel, Josephat, Rose,

Asha, Lynn, Linet, Violet, Ida, Selma, Paulynn, Cynthia, Dalifa, Mary, Irene, Maureen, Josephine, and Mamma Greggo. Thank you for your hospitality, for the courage and beauty with which you told your stories. Thank you for inviting me back. A piece of my heart will always remain with you at KGSA. This book in no way does justice to the strength of your persons or the magic of the family that is KGSA. I hope that, in some small way, this version of the story brings you honor.

Jamie, *Dada*, I am so lucky that this story brought us together. Your wisdom inspires me and your friendship is one of the greatest I've known. Thank you also to Jake Naughton for your brilliant pictures and your gorgeous heart. Thank you to KGSA's U.S. family who supported me and this project in so many ways, especially Shaun Lamory, Ellen Weber, Mookie Tierney, Matty Brandes, Sean Rush, Becky Albright, Matt Mussel, Cathy Huber, and Martha Johnson.

To the stunning faculty at Sarah Lawrence: I am still amazed when I dream back to my M.F.A. days and revel in the fact that you took me and my writing seriously. To Alice Truax, the best in the business, thank you for guiding me through my clunky thesis that, as you astutely pointed out, would become the notes for this book. To Verlyn Klinkenborg, who taught me how to write a sentence, thank you. And to Jo Ann Beard, who taught me that when your body forces you out of bed at 4:00 a.m. to write, you are headed in the right direction, thank you for reminding me that *it takes years to write a book.* Vijay Seshadri's strategic criticisms whispered in my ear and made me better to this day. Suzanne Gardinier taught me that doing nothing is part of the creative process, and that it is okay to sit and think for as long as it takes. And of course, thanks to Gerry Albarelli, the oral history master.

My colleagues at Sarah Lawrence enriched my life so deeply. Robbie Oxnard Bent, Katherine Reece, and Dakin Parker, our lunches grew my heart as well as my writing. Thank you for your friendship, encouragement, and constructive criticism. Catherine Hull, your tender companionship makes me strong. Margueya Novick, your sharp brilliance and wit are a breath of fresh air. Jennie Gruber, knowing you makes me a better person. You astound me.

Andy Brown, thank you yet again. Your big brain and heart were the perfect combination for taking in an early draft and offering me clarity on how to move the story forward. This was no small task and indeed ensured the story's improvement. Claire DeBerg, thank you for your deep investment in my writing. I was feeling alone as a writer in Minnesota, and then you appeared. Your skill, wit, energy, and art breathed life back into my writing and me. I am so grateful.

There is writing, and then there is publishing. Thank you so much to my lovely and fierce agent, Dawn Frederick, and the whole crew at Red Sofa Literary. Thank you for seeing me and advocating for this story. Thank you to Laura Duane and Viva Editions for working with me with diligence, spirit, and skill, and putting my book out into the world with style. Laura honored my story by reading it first as a compassionate woman and then as a sharp editor.

Molly Mjolsness, Chrissy Storlie, Steph Smith, Jessica Epple, Soren Poffenberger, Kirsten Patterson, Michelle Johnson, Amelia McGuinley, Heidi Barr, Tessa Lasswell, Michele Rae, and the entire Suds Committee, thank you for helping me be vulnerable and claim my desires for this project late in the game when I was weary. You were kind enough to know when to ask how the book was coming and when not to. You carried me through to the other side.

To my siblings who continue to love me and keep me humble, thank you for supporting me and KGSA in quiet and sustaining ways. Thank you to my parents, who prioritized excellent education in my childhood and supported my body, mind, and spirit in ways that led me to be a person who writes.